CONCEPT-BASED
INSTRUCTION

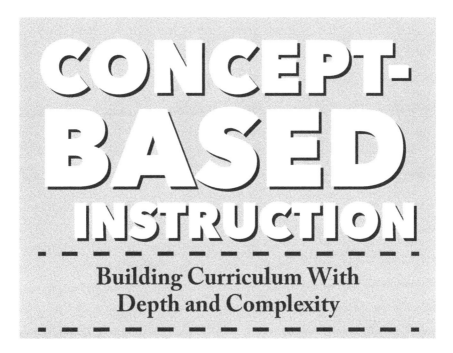

CONCEPT-BASED INSTRUCTION

Building Curriculum With Depth and Complexity

Brian E. Scott, Ed.D.

Routledge
Taylor & Francis Group

NEW YORK AND LONDON

First published in 2020 by Prufrock Press Inc.

Published in 2021 by Routledge
605 Third Avenue, New York, NY 10017
2 Park Square, Milton Park, Abingdon, Oxon OX14 4RN

Routledge is an imprint of the Taylor & Francis Group, an informa business.

Cover design by Micah Benson and layout design by Shelby Charette

Library of Congress Control Number:2019954615

ISBN-13: 978-1-0321-4234-0 (hbk)
ISBN-13: 978-1-6182-1887-2 (pbk)

DOI: 10.4324/9781003233770

Table of Contents

Introduction

Concept-based teaching was something I found unexpectedly. During my 20 years in the classroom I taught mainly intermediate grades. I started out as a general education classroom teacher and finished my classroom career teaching gifted and talented students in about every arrangement imaginable: before school, after school, weekly pull-out, multiage, self-contained, and cluster. As someone who is always eager to learn new ideas, I became a follower of Carol Ann Tomlinson and really respected her sensible ways to address various student learning needs and still maintain academic rigor. My career started before the days of state academic standards, and I was considered to be one of the most challenging and unyielding teachers in the building, mainly because that was the way I remembered the teachers who made the biggest impact on my own learning. Those teachers cared for my classmates and me but also had a firm hand in what they expected us to learn and what they thought we needed to know, whether it was in a textbook or not.

About halfway through my time in the classroom, I transitioned to a unique opportunity in my district as a high-ability teacher. Part of this change involved the implementation of specialized curriculum. Units of study were based on the collaborative work of Treffinger, Hohn, and Feldhusen (1979) in the handbook *Reach Each You Teach*. Units were focused on content objectives, process levels, learner characteristics, learning activities, and evaluation procedures. These were

1

DOI:10.4324/9781003233770-1

not lesson plans. The focus was taking the major objectives and creating potential activities using Bloom's (1956) taxonomy.

Several years later I taught a license renewal workshop on differentiated instruction that included part of a day on brain-compatible learning. As I looked for materials primarily shared in print or interviews by Pat Wolfe, I found that the idea of big concepts through thematic teaching really resonated with me, and consequently with the teachers in the workshop. In *Brain Matters: Translating Research Into Classroom Matters*, Wolfe (2001) reminded teachers that thematic units, such as those focused on dinosaurs, apples, or rain forests, are designed with no apparent concepts. The class learns names of dinosaurs, makes apple pie, or decorates the classroom in a canopy style, but there is no deep learning. According to Wolfe, "It is often difficult to determine why the theme was chosen, let alone answer questions concerning the relevance or application of what teachers are teaching" (p. 133). In contrast, concept-based unit development connects subject matter, ties it together with abstract ideas, and applies it to real-world situations.

Two years prior to becoming a building administrator, I decided to plan my classroom using Wolfe's (2001) design. I had a cluster of high-ability students assigned to me, and I had training and some experience, but I had never created an environment that deliberately approached unit development and instruction in quite this way. I found it to be very transformative, and students produced evidence in multiple ways (e.g., discussions, projects, high-quality work). Although this instruction was intended to reach my high-ability cluster, I found that my on-grade-level students benefitted as well, including those with autism and emotional disabilities.

The impetus for writing this book came from my wife, who had been a second-grade teacher for 20 years and was suddenly moved to teach high-ability fourth graders identified in mathematics, English language arts, or both. I supported her in developing her environment using many of the elements outlined in this book. As someone who had never taught in this type of atmosphere before, she was able to develop a classroom that impressed others, including administrators, program directors, and colleagues who actually had formal training. She knew I was contemplating retirement and thinking about chronicling something from my varied years of experience to help educators and remain relevant in the field. She stated simply, "This is the book you need to write!"

As a professional educator and scholar, I continue to learn more from educational leaders in curriculum development. *Concept-Based Instruction: Building Curriculum With Depth and Complexity* is a synthesis of those experiences and increased knowledge. Throughout the rest of this book, the reader will see parallels to my previous experiences in unit development, especially the elements of instructional objectives, learning activities, and evaluation procedures. These would be similar to what content is expected to be learned, what learning experiences students will have to demonstrate the learning, and how teachers and students will know that learning has been accomplished.

How to Use This Book

Concept-Based Instruction is not necessarily a "how-to" book, but it certainly gives guidance based on the work of educational leaders with a complete example of concept-based planning from start to finish. It also provides organizational templates to assist with the process. The purpose of this book is to provide teachers and unit developers a framework for creating a rich and deep concept unit that gathers content, skills, and understandings across learning institution subject matter. My hope is to give teachers a tool to accomplish something I did through trial and error and the feedback I received from others.

The first chapter introduces how I came to embrace the thinking and philosophy of high-quality curriculum development, pedagogy, and instructional practices. Principles of differentiated instruction may also be found in this chapter. *Differentiated instruction* was a term I had not formally heard until I was asked to help lead a summer retreat for my school on the topic in 1998. I was asked because I was regularly observed using differentiation in my classroom. I managed to get my hands on a book and a series of professional development videos facilitated by Tomlinson and published by the Association for Supervision and Curriculum Development (Kiernan & Bloom, 1997). As small as this step might have seemed, it probably had the greatest impact on my career. This professional development series served as the backbone of a popular summer workshop I created at a local university. It also expanded my understanding of curriculum development and its importance. Using Grant Wiggins and Jay McTighe's (2005) *Understanding by Design* for lesson planning allowed me to go deeper and be more intentional with instruction. Later I experienced the ideas of other thought leaders, including H. Lynn Erickson.

Chapter 2 takes the reader through the curriculum mapping process by considering the work of Heidi Hayes Jacobs. Instructional professionals should have a deep understanding and accurate interpretation of the subject and grade-level standards, including anything added by the district. The chapter is written using the Common Core State Standards (CCSS) for English Language Arts. The example utilized in the subsequent chapters is written at the fifth-grade level. Because the CCSS for Literacy in History/Social Studies, Science, and Technical Subjects begin at sixth grade, the units draw from the College, Career, and Civic Life (C3) Framework for Social Studies State Standards (National Council for the Social Studies [NCSS], 2013), along with the National Curriculum Standards for Social Studies (NCSS, 2010) and the Next Generation Science Standards.

In the third chapter teachers will discover what themes run across the grade-level curriculum maps in the subjects of English language arts, social studies, and science. Mathematics may be included as it might support these subjects. There is certainly potential to include mathematics as a complement to the other three, but it was not included as a major part of this book due its progressive and building nature. Ancillary subjects, such music, global studies, visual art, and physical education, may also be included, but schools may want to start with the core subjects and add others in the following years.

Chapters 4 and 5 integrate what students are to know, understand, and be able to do (KUD). Unit developers determine the long-term essential questions and enduring understandings (Wiggins & McTighe, 2005). These are extended through a fifth-grade sample unit identifying levels of Bloom's revised taxonomy (Anderson & Krathwohl, 2001) with Webb's (1999) Depth of Knowledge. Examples of student learning are present in several of the included tables.

The Appendix contains resources for teachers to develop their own units, including ideas of conceptual themes and templates for organizing yearly plans, 6-week units, and weekly maps. These resources maintain a focus on what students are to know, understand, and do. They also maintain a focus on the overarching essential questions and enduring understandings and allow opportunities for differentiation.

Chapter 1

Concept-Based Unit Design
Leading Instructional Philosophies

Part of being a teacher is improving your craft. There are many experts in the field of education in a variety of areas: diversity, curriculum, one-to-one implementation, social-emotional learning, etc. With so much to consider, it's no wonder that schools, administrators, and teachers feel overwhelmed. As educators look for approaches that will fix the problems in their schools, they are often faced with poorly planned implementation, shifting strategies, and quick-changing ideas to try—without ever giving last month's initiative enough time to determine instructional or learning effectiveness.

Concept-based curriculum is an approach that breaks down the silos of specific subject areas and brings them together through a broad-based theme. It provides higher level thinking and makes cross-curricular connections. Students not only learn facts and specific information, but also find answers to questions about why and how the content is important.

This book demonstrates how to blend many of these ideas in a disciplined format. Although every attempt has been made to stay true to the philosophical framework of the prestigious educational leaders discussed, this book is a synthesis of these works and will result in a slightly different interpretation of these ideas. The reader will notice that the format is gradual as opposed to being rapid, confusing, and frustrating; this ensures that practitioners can delve into new ideas at a pace that ensures success. Teachers quickly abandon ideas or become

DOI:10.4324/9781003233770-2

frustrated when something is implemented too quickly or without deliberate thought.

As with any promising idea, it is necessary to create a plan and stay the course with minor adjustments along the way. Often educators may neglect to reflect on the practice being implemented. If there is research to support complex implementation, then there must also be time built in to give it a chance. Starting with curriculum mapping and ending with thinking skills, teachers will learn how to include concept-based unit development and backward design to create deeper and more relevant learning. The works of prolific educators Carol Ann Tomlinson, John Hattie, Robert Marzano, and Richard DuFour will be reviewed to support the practice, development, and depth of these ideas.

Curriculum Mapping: Heidi Hayes Jacobs

Many schools and districts have gone through the "unpacking" of the standards—a process that adds clarity regarding the interpretation of rigor. The process of digging deeply into each standard and determining what skills need to be implicitly and explicitly taught is critical. This process can lead to determining what prerequisite skills are required before students are ready to learn new skills. Jacobs (1997), the premier expert, defined the process of curriculum mapping in this way:

> Curriculum mapping is a procedure for collecting data about the actual curriculum in a school district using the school calendar as an organizer. Data are gathered in a format that allows each teacher to present an overview of his or her students' actual learning experiences. The fundamental purpose of mapping is communication. The composite of each teacher's map in a building or district provides efficient access to a K–12 curriculum perspective both vertically and horizontally. Mapping is not presented as what *ought* to happen but what *is* happening during the course of a school year. Data offer an overview perspective rather than a daily classroom perspective. (p. 61)

Curriculum mapping serves as a series of steps for deciding what curriculum is necessary and then monitoring the planned curriculum (O'Malley, 1982). This process, which originally made use of index cards and charts, can now be completed in an electronic format, although many teachers appreciate having a large image and being able to physically move cards (or sticky notes) within the diagram. The concepts communicated by Jacobs (1997) highlight the importance of starting with this practice to look for gaps and overlaps throughout the year in all core subject areas (literacy, mathematics, writing/language, social studies, and science). Additional ancillary subjects should be included. Table 2.1 in Chapter 2 demonstrates an example of an integrated map to assist with better understanding.

Concept-Based Curriculum: H. Lynn Erickson

Once the year has been mapped out, the next step would be to identify what students are expected to know, understand, and be able to do in each area. The concept-based unit objectives extend the knowing, understanding, and actions in order to make connections to higher thoughts. A broad-based theme is used to connect multiple subjects. Throughout the implementation, students think deeper as they experience curricula and are guided to make connections in multiple ways.

In a recent book on concept-based curriculum, Erickson, Lanning, and French (2017) introduced the idea of including process skills, especially in writing. Figure 1.1 is an adapted version of the concept map. Starting at the bottom of the lower triangle, the skills and facts are at the basic level. These come together to create a topic, such as grammar or ecosystems, at the top of this bottom triangle. Teachers can then review the topics to look for a shared concept shown in the rectangle, such as "a cause creates an effect, reward, or consequence." Students then expand from generalizations to learn principles or interact with theories. Teachers need to be prepared to not have a perfect or correct answer. When the class wrestles with the concepts together, the knowledge gained is respectful of others' ideas, requires justification for the line of thinking, and causes students to take on different perspectives.

Components of Erickson's Concept Map

Theories are evidence-based and occur in nature or are a specific behavior. Examples would be "The conspiracy of the assassination of President John F. Kennedy" and "Global warming is destroying the polar ice caps."

Concept-Based Instruction

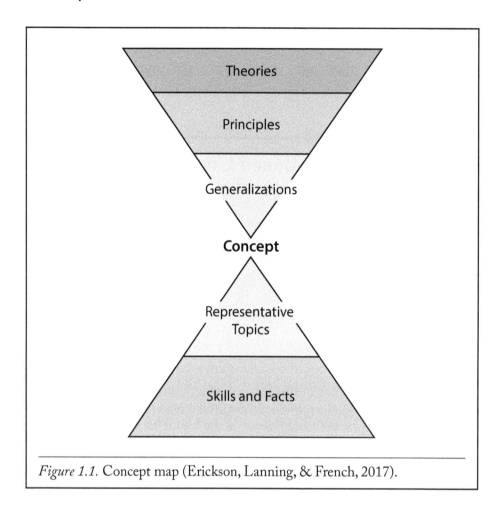

Figure 1.1. Concept map (Erickson, Lanning, & French, 2017).

Principles state a relationship between two or more concepts: "The Earth revolves around the sun and is kept in orbit due to gravity" and "All even numbers end in 0, 2, 4, 6, and 8, and divide in half evenly and without a remainder."

Generalizations are the "big ideas" from a learning experience and are related to the topics of study and concepts. These are critical learnings and understandings. Examples would include "Different factor pairs can create the same product" and "Rules and laws are necessary for order in a civilization."

Concepts are transferrable to other disciplines, are intangible because they are ideas, and are commonly understood. For the purpose of this book, they are broad-based and include examples like "Relationships," "Structure," and "Culture."

Representative Topics are found within a content area or subject, such as "Westward Movement," "Space," and "Trigonometry."

Skills and Facts are determined by the content standards of the state.

— — — — — — — — — — — — — — — —

After reviewing the aforementioned theories, principles, generalizations, concepts, topics, facts, and skills, some adjustments might be made to put logical topics in the core subject areas to create cohesive conceptual themes without causing a disconnect of progression. This part of the unit design could take the largest amount of time to accomplish. Having a logical, understandable, and detailed curriculum map will expedite this process.

Essential Questions and Enduring Understandings: Grant Wiggins and Jay McTighe

Wiggins and McTighe introduced Understanding by Design in the late 1990s. It is a framework for improving student achievement in which the teacher is viewed as a designer of the learning with close attention paid to the curriculum standards (Wiggins & McTighe, 2005). Teachers determine how students are to learn and engage with the material, and align assessments to match the goals and expectations. They plan for what students are able to know, understand, and do. Wiggins and McTighe identified these as Stage 1, or the desired results. The goal is to make the learning experiences transferrable to other disciplines and to real-life situations.

Stage 2 involves the evidence of learning, which can be established in several ways (Wiggins & McTighe, 2005). Will it be through a performance-based task at the end of a unit that demonstrates an application of the targeted learning in a new and real-life situation? Will it be through a formative short-term quiz or test, or will it be a report or presentation? Through questions like these, teachers must think like assessors. Wiggins and McTighe identified true understanding in one of the following ways, also known as the six facets of learning:

1. explaining concepts, principles, and processes;
2. interpreting by making sense of the text, a set of data, and experiences;
3. applying in new contexts;
4. seeing a different perspective or point of view;
5. demonstrating empathy through taking the position of the other person; and
6. having self-awareness of what the learning experience was like.

Concept-Based Instruction

Deciding which facet to implement depends on the subject and content being learned.

Once these elements are identified, Stage 3, the unit plan or learning plan, can begin (Wiggins & McTighe, 2005). Teachers may know this stage as backward design. Educators decide what evidence will prove that students have met the learning goals. To truly have a deep understanding, students need to be given numerous opportunities to interact with the information, with the teacher taking on the role of facilitator and coach rather than dispenser of information. These steps are compatible to those used in designing a concept-based unit.

Much has been written about Erickson's (2012) expertise in working with the International Baccalaureate (IB) curriculum design and how comparable it is to Wiggins and McTighe's (2005) essential questions and enduring understandings. Although each subject area can have its own essential questions and enduring understandings, connections can be made across multiple subject areas with deeper meaning. Wiggins and McTighe's essential questions and enduring understandings serve as references for student thinking, discussion, conversation, and written word. Units should take place over several weeks and include checkpoints along the way to ensure that the complexity that students will experience is connected to the learning. Emphasis will then be placed on the result to demonstrate evidence of what students have gained.

Drake and Burns (2004) summarized Wiggins and McTighe's three stages of curriculum planning in their book, *Meeting Standards Through Integrated Curriculum*. Wiggins and McTighe developed these stages to help teachers with the development of the unit and stay focused on the standards, thus securing the evidence of the learning. Wiggins and McTighe determined that the following questions may be used (as cited in Drake & Burns, 2004):

◈ For identifying the purpose and desired results:
  - What is worthy and required for understanding?
  - How will students be different at the end of the unit?

◈ For reviewing the standards to determine how to use them in an interdisciplinary framework:
  - Can standards be organized in meaningful ways that cut across the curriculum?

◈ For securing acceptable proof of learning:
  - What is evidence of understanding?

◈ For deciding the experiences that lead to desired results:
  - What learning experiences promote understanding and lead to desired results? (p. 33)

Benjamin Bloom's Taxonomy

Bloom's (1956) taxonomy has been use as a cognitive hierarchical structure of higher order thinking since the mid-1950s to create assessments, develop courses, plan lessons, evaluate the complexity of assignments, and establish project-based learning. Bloom classified the criteria from lowest to highest: knowledge, comprehension, application, analysis, synthesis, and evaluation. Bloom's taxonomy centers on the verbal action (e.g., create, define, compare, classify, estimate, describe) rather than the product that is evidence of the learning. Although teachers might include a specific verb in writing a lesson outcome, the end result could be at a lower level. One example would be, "How will my family *decide* on what to eat for dinner tonight?" The teacher's intent might be at the evaluative level of Bloom's taxonomy, but there is no mention of a set criteria as required. Without the criteria portion being included, this question is at an analysis level at best. To be at the higher level, it can be restated as, "*Using selected criteria*, how will my family *decide* on what to eat for dinner tonight?" Table 1.1 gives a brief list of verbs associated with each level to create learning objectives.

In 2001, Anderson and Krathwohl determined that synthesis should be placed at a higher level than evaluation, and renamed it *create* because of the creative thinking involved of taking knowledge and using it in a novel or unique way (see Figure 1.2). Since Bloom's death in 1999, psychologists have adjusted the six levels from nouns to verbs.

Norman Webb's Depth of Knowledge

Webb is a senior research scientist emeritus for the Wisconsin Center for Education Research at the University of Wisconsin-Madison. In conducting alignment studies, he has used his Depth of Knowledge (DOK) system. DOK is a language system developed through a curriculum approach that assumes multiple factors contribute to what is complex, including content area attributes rather than only the verb or action.

In a research study conducted by Webb (1999), a panel of reviewers agreed that four levels were an adequate number for comparing the standards with the assessments for mathematics. The panel found Level 2 (Skill/Concept) was used most frequently and did not distinguish among the items and standards. The analysis helped the reviewers to clarify how they used the different levels:

◈ **Level 1 (Recall)** is the remembering of information. This would include facts, definitions, terms, or simple procedures. A mathematics example would be performing a simple algorithm or applying a formula. Simply

Table 1.1
Bloom's (1956) Taxonomy With Sample Verbs

Bloom's Level	Verbs
Evaluation (highest level)	assess, rate, appraise, evaluate, justify, defend, relate
Synthesis	create, arrange, combine, generate, formulate, design
Analysis	analyze, compare/contrast, break down, categorize, infer
Application	change, classify, demonstrate, schedule, sketch, solve
Comprehension	classify, describe, paraphrase, estimate, explain, summarize
Knowledge (lowest level)	define, duplicate, label, recall, recognize, reproduce

stated, it is one-step, well-defined, and procedural. In science, a simple experimental procedure including one or two steps should be coded as Level 1. Similar to the knowledge/remembering level of Bloom's taxonomy, key words that signify a Level 1 include *identify, recall, recognize, use,* and *measure*. Verbs such as *describe* and *explain* could be classified at different levels depending on what is being described and explained. These words would often fall in the classification of the comprehension/understanding level of Bloom's taxonomy.

❖ **Level 2 (Skill/Concept)** includes the action of some mental processing beyond a typical response. A Level 2 assessment item expects students to make some decisions as to how to approach the problem or activity. On the other hand, Level 1 requires students to demonstrate a rote response, such as performing a common mathematical algorithm, following a set procedure (like the steps of the scientific method), or completing a clearly defined series of steps. Similar to the comprehension/understanding level of Bloom's taxonomy, key words and phrases that generally distinguish a Level 2 item include *classify, organize, estimate, make observations, collect and display data,* and *compare data*. These actions suggest multiple steps. For example, to compare data requires one to first determine traits of the objects and then group or order the objects. Some action verbs, such as *explain, describe,* or *interpret*, could be classified at different levels depending on the object of the action. For example, if an item required students to explain how the tilt and rotation of the Earth around the sun affects the changes of seasons and the length of daylight hours, then this is considered Level 2. Interpreting information from

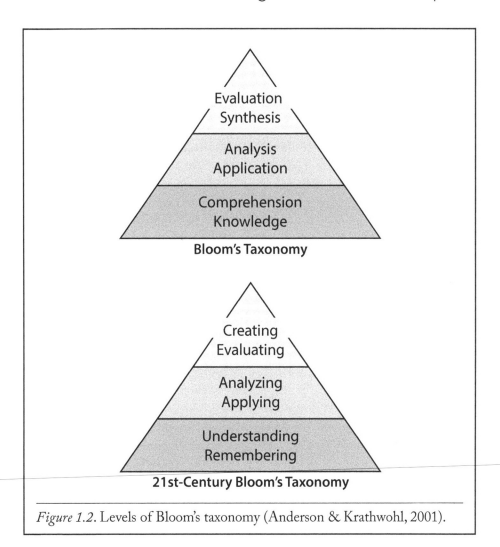

Evaluation
Synthesis

Analysis
Application

Comprehension
Knowledge

Bloom's Taxonomy

Creating
Evaluating

Analyzing
Applying

Understanding
Remembering

21st-Century Bloom's Taxonomy

Figure 1.2. Levels of Bloom's taxonomy (Anderson & Krathwohl, 2001).

a simple graph and reading information from the graph also are Level 2. Similar to DOK 1, this crosses over into a level of thinking closely aligned to Bloom's application level. Unlike the classification system of Bloom's taxonomy, a slight shift in the level of thinking changes in DOK. An example of Level 2 would be interpreting information from a complex graph that requires some decisions on what features of the graph need to be considered and how information from the graph can be collected. Students need to use reasoning skills or explain their thinking by interpreting the information. Caution is warranted in interpreting Level 2 as only skills. Some reviewers will interpret skills very narrowly as primarily numerical skills; such interpretation excludes from this level other skills, such as visualization skills and probability skills, which may be more complex simply because they are less common. A literacy skill repeatedly found in the Common Core State Standards is the citing of text evidence from a single resource. By the upper elementary grades, students are expected to draw conclusions by taking information from two different texts. As the type of text changes (e.g., comparing fiction with nonfiction), the complexity increases and moves to a strategic level of thinking found in Level 3.

❖ **Level 3 (Strategic Thinking)** requires reasoning, planning, using evidence, and a higher level of thinking than the previous two levels. In most instances, requiring students to explain and defend their thinking is Level 3. Activities that require students to make mathematical conjectures or inferences are also at this level. The cognitive demands at Level 3 are complex and abstract. Although this level generally will result in multiple answers, it is not the only level where this can occur. Multiple answers can be found at both Levels 1 and 2, but the task in Level 3 requires more demanding reasoning. Justifying the answer would most likely be Level 3. Other Level 3 activities include drawing conclusions from observations, such as recording phenomena in a science experiment; citing evidence and developing a logical argument for concepts from multiple media resources, including printed materials, speeches, poetry, and multimedia; explaining phenomena in terms of concepts; and using concepts to solve problems.

❖ **Level 4 (Extended Thinking)** requires complex reasoning, planning, developing, and thinking, most likely over an extended period of time. Taking the Level 3 example of interpreting scientific results and drawing conclusions about what they mean, a Level 4 task would require the student to design the activity posed with a specific question (e.g., Do plants require light in order to germinate? Does the level of exercise a mammal receives influence obesity? Why is structure important for order in a tall tale? What is the significance of "Give me liberty or give me death"?). The extended time period is not a distinguishing factor if the required work is only repetitive and does not require applying significant conceptual understanding and higher order thinking. In another example, a student takes the water temperature from a river each day for a month and then constructs a graph. This would be classified as a Level 2. However, if the student conducts a river study that requires taking into consideration a number of variables, this would be Level 4. At Level 4, the cognitive demands of the task should be high and the work very complex. The number of connections increases. DOK Level 4 ties closely to concept-based learning experiences because students are required to make several connections, relate ideas within the content area or among content areas, and select one approach among many alternatives for how the situation should be solved. Level 4 activities often take place over an extended period of time and cannot be assessed on statewide competency instruments that are often constrained by time. These activities include designing and conducting experiments; making connections between a finding and related concepts and phenomena; combining and synthesizing ideas into new concepts; and critiquing experimental designs.

To have the full range of cognitive thinking, educators should synthesize the work of Bloom and Webb to create levels of questioning and task complexity based on various forms of assessments and demonstrated readiness. This approach to unit writing deepens the thinking in classrooms as opposed to the surface-level coverage through traditional classroom texts, media materials, and worksheets. An example of this objective using this combination of Bloom and Webb might be: "After experiencing text and media information, students will identify the need for water, food, and air for survival at a predetermined level of mastery." This would be at the application level of Bloom's taxonomy because of the transfer of what students have learned about the importance of lifeforms having basic survival needs, but the DOK would be at a Level 1 or 2 because students are using limited resources provided by the teacher. Notice that there might not be one specific DOK level. The interpretation sometimes falls in two adjacent levels depending on how the objective is executed.

Hess, Jones, Carlock, and Walkup (2009) conducted a study of large-scale collections of student work samples analyzed using a cognitive rigor matrix, illustrating the multitude of curricular items aligned to each cell in the matrix. They drew the following conclusion from examining the two:

> Although related through their natural ties to the complexity of thought, Bloom's Taxonomy and Webb's DOK model differ in scope and application. Bloom's Taxonomy categorizes the cognitive skills required of the brain when faced with a new task, therefore describing the type of thinking processes necessary to answer a question. Depth of Knowledge, on the other hand, relates more closely to the depth of content understanding and scope of a learning activity, which manifests in the skills required to complete the task from inception to finale (e.g., planning, researching, drawing conclusions). (p. 4)

Table 1.2 is an example of cognitive rigor in the form of a matrix with curricular examples extracted. It is based on the matrix developed by Hess et al. (2009).

Table 1.2
Cognitive Rigor With Curricular Examples

21st-Century Bloom's Taxonomy	Webb's Depth of Knowledge Levels			
	Recall and Reproduction (DOK 1)	Skills and Concepts (DOK 2)	Strategic Thinking or Reasoning (DOK 3)	Extended Thinking (DOK 4)
Remember (define, duplicate, label, recall, recognize, reproduce)	◆ Define vocabulary. ◆ Label diagram accurately. ◆ Identify facts/ details.			
Understand (classify, describe, paraphrase, estimate, explain, summarize)	◆ Solve or evaluate an expression. ◆ Locate places on a map or graph. ◆ Compose simple sentences.	◆ Summarize the plot of a story. ◆ Classify colors as primary, secondaray, or tertiary. ◆ Estimate mathematical equations.	◆ Write a composition with multiple paragraphs. ◆ Describe the theme of a story. ◆ Generalize science concepts.	◆ Write a biography using multiple sources. ◆ Generalize how two events in history influenced later events.

Table 1.2, continued

21st-Century Bloom's Taxonomy	Webb's Depth of Knowledge Levels			
	Recall and Reproduction (DOK 1)	Skills and Concepts (DOK 2)	Strategic Thinking or Reasoning (DOK 3)	Extended Thinking (DOK 4)
Apply (analyze, compare/contrast, breakdown, categorize, infer)	◆ Follow directions or steps to a procedure. ◆ Use a mathematical algorithm accurately. ◆ Apply information in a graphic template.	◆ Write a paragraph with correct structure and mechanics. ◆ Respond to comprehension questions regarding main ideas/details and cause/effect relationships. ◆ Respond to math story problems with accuracy.	◆ Complete predesigned science experiments. ◆ Survey a sample group and organize the data into a graph. ◆ Compare an element of two texts and create a T-chart.	◆ Research a service project on a budget of $1,000,000, complete with expense report and detailed description.
Analyze (change, classify, demonstrate, schedule, sketch, solve)	◆ Gather information from a table or graph. ◆ Interpret the information conveyed on a map, table, or graph.	◆ Revise word choice in writing. ◆ Solve multistep math problems. ◆ Classify types of rocks based on characteristics.	◆ Use a Venn diagram to compare two characters, events, or mathematical concepts (e.g., multiplication and addition). ◆ Continue a mathematical pattern.	◆ Research a local environmental problem and work with a team to develop a practical solution. ◆ Conduct a survey on a topic, and organize and interpret the results.

Table 1.2, continued

21st-Century Bloom's Taxonomy	Webb's Depth of Knowledge Levels			
	Recall and Reproduction (DOK 1)	Skills and Concepts (DOK 2)	Strategic Thinking or Reasoning (DOK 3)	Extended Thinking (DOK 4)
Evaluate (assess, rate, appraise, evaluate, justify, defend, relate)			◆ Defend an opinion from two different perspectives. ◆ Argue which mathematical algorithm is the best one for a particular situation.	◆ Create your own platform to be elected for class president that includes 3–5 issues worthy of a debate. ◆ Justify a character's decision in a piece of literature based on class-created criteria.
Create (create, arrange, combine, generate, formulate, design)	◆ List topical ideas or concepts.	◆ Produce or theorize based on interpretations or prior experiences.	◆ Create information within one cause or text. ◆ Devise a new problem. ◆ Build a multifaceted model for a given condition.	◆ Integrate information from various sources to solve a problem. ◆ Create a board game based on a historical event or a novel.

Connecting to Other Contemporary Ideas and Research

At the end of each chapter, connections will be made to related educational leaders' research findings, successful practices, or philosophies that have been frequently embraced. This demonstrates how concept-based instruction relates to other educational theories. Tomlinson's differentiated instruction, DuFour's professional learning communities, Marzano's essential skills, and Hattie's visible learning support concept-based unit development. These are separate from the integral components of Jacobs's curriculum mapping, Wiggins and McTighe's Understanding by Design, and, of course, Erickson's concept-based learning. After teachers have the units reasonably created based on the previous sections, they should look for ways to have continuous instructional improvement implementing these educational contributions.

Differentiated Instruction: Carol Ann Tomlinson

In *How to Differentiate Instruction in Academically Diverse Classrooms* (3rd ed.), Tomlinson (2017) outlined the following strategies for differentiation instruction:

◈ **Learning centers:** These can be stations or collections of materials learners use to explore topics or practice skills. Teachers can adjust learning center tasks to readiness levels or learning styles. Teachers use materials and activities addressing a wide range of reading levels, learning profiles, and interest. Activities vary from simple to complex, abstract to concrete, and structured to open-ended. They provide an opportunity for students to close gaps on missing or unclear conceptions on content or skills, or to have an opportunity for deeper thinking or acceleration. A record-keeping system should be in place to track what types of work students experience, with a focus on the quality and completion level of the work (Tomlinson, 2014).

◈ **Compacting:** This is a three-step process that (1) assesses what a student knows about material to be studied and what the student still needs to master, (2) plans for learning what is not known and excuses the student from what is known, and (3) plans for free time to be spent in enriched or accelerated study.

◈ **Tiered assignments:** In a heterogeneous classroom, a teacher uses varied levels of activities to ensure that students explore ideas at a level that builds on their prior knowledge and prompts continued growth. Student groups use varied approaches to explore essential ideas. At times these may look similar to varying questions.

◈ **Varying questions:** In class discussions and on tests, teachers vary the sorts of questions posed to learners based on their readiness, interests, and learning styles. These types of questions may also vary on tiered assignments.

◈ **Flexible grouping:** Students are part of many different groups—and also work alone—based on the match of the task to student readiness for instruction, interest, or learning style. Teachers may create skills-based groups that are heterogeneous or homogeneous in readiness level. Sometimes students select work groups, and sometimes teachers select them. In addition, these groups are sometimes purposeful and sometimes random.

◈ **Contracts:** These take a number of forms that begin with an agreement between student and teacher. The teacher grants certain freedoms and choices about how a student will complete tasks, and the student agrees to use the freedoms appropriately in designing and completing work according to specifications. Contracts would include students completing a personalized list of tasks in a specified time. The teacher creates an agenda that will last the student 2–3 weeks that includes special instructions for each task and allows the student to determine the order of the tasks. Time is often set aside (daily, weekly, etc.) to work on agenda activities. As a common support to small-group instruction, this design allows the teacher to monitor the progress of individual students and instruct small groups of students having difficulty with similar tasks or skills (Tomlinson, 2014).

◈ **Pretesting:** This technique is used to find out what a student knows and does not know prior to formal instruction. This form of assessment is often the driving force in determining how, why, and what type of differentiated instruction will take place.

In *The Differentiated Classroom: Responding to the Needs of All Learners* (2nd ed.), Tomlinson (2014) also discussed the following strategies:

◈ **Small groups:** These are instructional groups that draw upon the individual strengths of a student. These might include allowing for a variety of solutions and solution routes, including topics that are of particular interest to students, having a real-world connection, integrating reading and writing, use various sources of media, or requiring different talents to complete a whole task.

◈ **Independent research:** Students select a topic from a larger theme in the curriculum and investigate independently. Somewhat like with the learning contract, the teacher and student agree on the plan with the teacher providing guidance. The student has the chance to develop more expertise on the topic and learn how to become an independent investigator.

◈ **Learning profile:** The teacher uses students' learner profiles to plan instruction. Students are given the choice of avenues to begin studying the topic or concept, either individually or in small groups, after the teacher presents the subject matter. This approach considers auditory, visual, and kinesthetic modalities as well as limited verbal capabilities.

◈ **Problem-based learning:** The teacher presents students with a problem that is complex or unclear. Students then seek additional information. The process includes defining the problem, locating and using valid resources, determining the success criteria for making decisions about solutions, posing a solution, communicating that solution to others, and assessing the solution's effectiveness. This strategy is related to Future Problem Solving Program International, a nonprofit organization that organizes academic competitions. Students apply critical thinking and problem-solving skills to hypothetical future situations.

◈ **Group investigation:** This approach is similar to independent study but takes place in a larger group. The teacher still guides students through the investigation of a topic related to something else being studied in the class. Respect is still given to individual members of the groups because students are divided by learner interest. The teacher assists in planning and carrying out the investigation, presenting the findings, and evaluating outcomes.

◈ **Choice boards:** Students choose assignments from a choice board, which is designed with pockets containing varied tasks and instructions based on the core concept being taught. Students choose a topic suited to their multiple intelligences, learning styles, or readiness level from a row or options.

Beecher and Sweeny (2008) published a research study on differentiated instruction indicating that on state achievement tests over a 7-year period, Asian students improved by more than 60%, African American students by more than 20%, and White and Hispanic students by more than 5% after receiving differentiated instruction. Students qualifying for free or reduced lunch improved by nearly 30% on state achievement tests. In another publication, Scott (2012) concluded that students with above-average ability were found to benefit from differentiated instruction at a significant level.

Concept-Based Instruction

Professional Learning Communities: Richard DuFour

A professional learning community (PLC) is a school environment in which teachers work collaboratively in purposefully designed groups to improve student achievement with support from the school administrator (Ontario Principals' Council, 2008).

The term *PLC* can mean different things to different people. It has been created to represent everything from special initiative teams to staffs engaged in learning together. DuFour (2004) stated:

> People use this term to describe every imaginable combination of individuals with an interest in education—a grade-level teaching team, a school committee, a high school department, an entire school district, a state department of education, a national professional organization, and so on. In fact, the term has been used so ubiquitously that it is in danger of losing all meaning. (p. 6)

PLCs come out of a constructivist framework (Bruner, 1996). Constructivism is based on the belief that learning occurs as learners are actively involved in a process of meaning and knowledge construction as opposed to passively receiving information. Constructivism fosters critical thinking and creates motivated learners. The development of PLCs was based on the idea that, through dialogue, teachers can form a network of understanding or a community of others with whom they can learn and share (McLaughlin & Talbert, 2001). As the idea of teachers working collaboratively in teams has evolved, collaborative focus has shifted from schoolwide teams preoccupied with general operations to grade-level and subject-centered teams whose mission is to improve student achievement.

Researchers at the Center on Organization and Restructuring of Schools at the University of Wisconsin-Madison (Newmann & Wehlage, 1995) examined the most valuable way to restructure schools in order to increase student achievement from 1990 through 1995. The researchers scrutinized data during this period from more than 1,500 elementary, middle, and high schools throughout the United States. They also conducted field research in 44 schools in 22 districts in 16 states. Newmann and Wehlage recognized that there was no "magic bullet" for consistent improvement that worked in all areas consistently. They did find that restructured schools that functioned as a PLC were the most successful. These schools frequently had high levels of pedagogy and also functioned better at increasing student achievement. The researchers cautioned that building these learning communities required a well-defined mission and trusting conditions.

Additionally, Lee, Smith, and Croninger (1995) released a report on successful school restructuring endeavors. Their study involved 11,000 students in 820 schools throughout the United States. Their findings were characterized by professional learning communities frequently engaging students in higher levels of tasks, a goal of concept-based unit development. In these schools, described as professional learning communities, teachers and students were more devoted to the goals and mission of the school, and the staff worked closely together to improve classroom instruction. In addition, these PLCs produced increased levels of student achievement in all core subject areas. Achievement gaps between student subgroups also decreased.

The strength of PLCs is assessing whether students have learned the essential curriculum. The essential curriculum is defined as the priority standards—the most critical of the CCSS. Teachers work with colleagues to develop a series of common formative assessments that are aligned with priority standards and district curriculum guides. PLCs establish the specific proficiency levels that each student is to meet. Teams administer their common formative assessments multiple times throughout the school year and analyze the results together. Teachers use the results to inform and improve their individual and collective practice, to identify students who need additional time and support for learning, and to help students monitor their own progress toward agreed-upon priority standards (DuFour, DuFour, Eaker, & Many, 2006; Schmoker, 2011).

Because many schools have adopted the PLC practice, it makes a lot of sense that concept-based teaching and unit development be a part of the process. As pointed out earlier, teachers are working in collaboration to map out the year and define what students should know, understand, and be able to do. Assessment, regardless of what tool is used, defines how educators will know whether students have learned or not learned the expectations of the unit. A critical role in determining the instructional approach is considering the various ways the learning can take place with the level of differentiation based on the desired outcomes and focus of the PLC.

Strategies That Work: Robert Marzano

Marzano has influenced instructional practices in education over the last several years. He has presented a meta-analysis on instructional practices, classroom management, and teacher effectiveness, as well as publications on assessment and grading practices, and continues to engage in varied and ongoing topics. One of the first and most embraced was his presentation of the nine instructional strategies. These strategies are (Marzano, Pickering, & Pollock, 2001):

1. identifying similarities and differences (compare, classify, and create metaphors, analogies, and nonlinguistic or graphic representations),

2. summarizing and note-taking (eliminate unnecessary information, substitute some information, keep important information, write/rewrite, and analyze information),
3. reinforcing effort and providing recognition (use symbolic recognition rather than just tangible rewards),
4. homework and practice (vary the amount of homework—less at the elementary level, more at the secondary level; keep parent involvement in homework to a minimum and brief),
5. nonlinguistic recommendations (use graphic representations, models, mental pictures, drawings, pictographs, and hands-on activities),
6. cooperative learning (limit use of ability groups, keep groups small, apply strategy consistently without overusing, and assign roles and responsibilities in groups),
7. setting objectives and providing feedback (make specific but flexible goals with corrective, timely, and specific feedback),
8. generating and testing hypotheses (use inductive and deductive strategies through problem solving, investigation, invention, experimental inquiry, and decision making), and
9. cues, questions, and advance organizers (use ample wait time before accepting responses, focusing on what is important and useful).

In a 2009 issue of *Phi Delta Kappan*, Marzano clarified that his findings were never intended to be a narrowed list of approaches. Marzano stated:

> The important message here is that providing feedback to teachers regarding effective instruction necessitates articulating a broad array of strategies organized into a comprehensive framework. To adapt a well-worn cliché, the whole is "more valid" than the sum of its parts. . . . I tried to provide a view of how a comprehensive framework of teaching might be organized. (p. 32)

A specific instructional strategy is effective only when used in the particular situation for which it was designed. Teachers should look for natural opportunities to implement the most appropriate strategies. Marzano went on to state the following regarding these "high yield strategies" as coined by schools and districts:

> The term "high yield" encourages educators to assume that strategies identified in the research are guaranteed to work. For the record, I've tried to avoid using this term over the last decade. . . . [W]e used the term "high probability" strategies. . . . If you

examine the research on classroom strategies, you'll find that some have an average effect size that's larger than others. (p. 34)

Teachers can find certain strategies are more appropriate for selected lessons, certain stages in the learning, and specific learning goals.

In this same article, Marzano (2009) cited the work of Hattie, a professor and director of the Melbourne Education Research Institute at the University of Melbourne, Australia. Marzano wrote:

> Hattie examined 146,142 effect sizes from studies on educational strategies, programs, and practice. From this, he identified 138 variables, many of which were instructional strategies and school- or district-level innovations. He even ordered them from highest to lowest in terms of effect sizes. Feedback was one of the highest ranked instructional strategies. (p. 34)

Hattie ranked feedback in the top 20 of the 250 strategies analyzed. In addition to teaching, he also looked into the categories of curricula, school, home, and student.

Visible Learning: John Hattie

In *Visible Learning for Teachers: Maximizing Impact on Learning*, Hattie (2012) wrote about three areas:

1. Teacher roles and sources of ideas; lesson planning, including preparation and implementation (includes prior student achievement, learning targets defined, adjusting for different rates of learning, and teachers collaborating to improve chances for success).
2. Learning goals and the importance and appropriateness of feedback; closing the lesson (includes teacher monitoring of the goals of the lesson and unit, how to reach those objectives, and anticipating how to respond to what comes next in terms of reaching the goals).
3. The mindframes of teachers, school leaders, and systems:
   - Teachers have an impact on student learning.
   - Assessment informs a teacher's next instructional steps.
   - Students and peers provide the best feedback for teacher progress and feedback.
   - Teachers believe in the ability to be a positive change agent for improvement.
   - Teachers expect the best out of themselves.

- There is a creation of mutual respect for feedback between instructors and students.
- Students learn best when there is an atmosphere of purposeful conversational exchange.
- Teachers model how high impact looks from the beginning of the year.
- Teachers allow mistakes and facilitate the learning from others with trust and relationships.
- Teachers create an atmosphere of constant learning.

Through his research, Hattie found that the last statement should be the foundation for what decisions a school makes. His meta-analysis indicated that teacher self-efficacy has the greatest impact on learning. Creating an open mind of growth in teachers and students with a focus on continuous learning has the greatest impact on high achievement.

Although this book focuses on the elements needed for the creation of concept-based instruction—including mapping, framing the unit, and implementing a high level of rigor—each of the following chapters also includes one or more of the theories of Bloom, Webb, Tomlinson, DuFour et al., Marzano, and Hattie as they pertain to creating and deepening the unit development. As the reader interacts with this work, it is quite possible a new connection will be made through one or more of the lenses created by these educational game changers.

Chapter 2
Mapping the Cross-Curricular Year

The process of curriculum mapping lays out the content and skills that will be taught, usually for the year. Depending on the situation, this work can be done at the classroom, school, or district level. Teachers are often so concerned with the day-to-day lessons that they do not always have the time or ability to think about the big picture. Mapping communicates the curricular plan in a procedural manner and provides an opportunity to monitor it (O'Malley, 1982). Although at first it may seem to just be an extended lesson plan, curricular mapping can guarantee little to no gaps or overlapping of curriculum at a grade level or from one grade level to another. It also creates alignment and provides potential connections across various subjects. Content in science and social studies is often experienced by students for brief periods of time, such as a couple of weeks. Skills-based subjects, like mathematics and writing, often spiral and expand as the year moves on. Reinforcing these skills in a curriculum map guarantees the proper balance of planning and practice, and vertically informs the adjacent grade levels of each one's role in students' education. Working together in this manner provides teachers ownership, self-efficacy, and clear instructional goals.

Curriculum maps assist in providing an overview of the curriculum students will learn and experience for the year. In concept-based unit development, educators should look at the common themes across content areas and potentially move elements to better complement other content areas in a cross-curricular

DOI:10.4324/9781003233770-3

manner. By doing so, the unit designer is setting up a more connected and richer learning experience for the student. Standards are a part of the curriculum, but they are not the curriculum. This is particularly evident when skills embedded in the standards are repeated at various points during the year. Understanding this is especially important when today's standards are written with such complexity and multiple layers.

English Language Arts

Tables 2.1A–2.1F provide a map of fifth-grade reading and English language arts using the CCSS. Note how the set of tables is divided into sections. Planning in a monthly structure or in interval sections of a year will help in the unit development process. Six-week units allow for adequate interaction with the subject matter and the overall concept without lacking depth due to being too brief. On the other hand, units lasting 9 weeks or more begin to drag and lose focus as well as become too cumbersome to manage. Teachers in classrooms on a grading period different from 6 weeks in length will need to consider how to combine or break apart the unit for the sake of assigning grades. Also, note that some standards in this set of tables, and other tables, have been abbreviated due to space.

If an elementary school or district is using a basal reading program, many of the units already have an overarching theme. Because they have a skill-building scope and sequence, these units potentially create a ready-made framework for teaching concepts. This framework would be an exception in building concept-based units.

Social Studies

Table 2.2 is a map of the social studies standards for fifth grade. This map complements the previous one, as both are humanities-based. Creating a map of the standards is one of the first steps in looking for common themes. Reviewing each of these themes and standards may promote movement for alignment purposes and integration. The social studies themes in the table use the standards and indicators from the C3 Framework for Social Studies States Standards.

In addition, the NCSS (2010) identified 10 interrelated themes addressed in social studies content. A school course in a social studies discipline is likely to touch on more than one theme. The 10 themes are:

Table 2.1A
Sample Fifth-Grade Curriculum Map of Repeated Yearlong
Skills for English Language Arts (Literacy)

RF.5.3 Know and apply grade-level phonics and word analysis skills in decoding words.
- ◆ RF.5.3.A Use combined knowledge of all letter-sound correspondences, syllabication patterns, and morphology (e.g., roots and affixes) to read accurately unfamiliar multisyllabic words in context and out of context.

RF.5.4 Read with sufficient accuracy and fluency to support comprehension.
- ◆ RF.5.4.A Read grade-level text with purpose and understanding.
- ◆ RF.5.4.B Read grade-level prose and poetry orally with accuracy, appropriate rate, and expression on successive readings.
- ◆ RF.5.4.C Use context to confirm or self-correct word recognition and understanding, rereading as necessary.

RL.5.4 Determine the meaning of words and phrases as they are used in a text, including figurative language such as metaphors and similes.

L.5.4 Determine or clarify the meaning of unknown and multiple-meaning words and phrases based on grade 5 reading and content, choosing flexibly from a range of strategies.
- ◆ L.5.4.A Use context (e.g., cause/effect relationships and comparisons in text) as a clue to the meaning of a word or phrase.
- ◆ L.5.4.B Use common, grade-appropriate Greek and Latin affixes and roots as clues to the meaning of a word (e.g., photograph, photosynthesis).
- ◆ L.5.4.C Consult reference materials (e.g., dictionaries, glossaries, thesauruses), both print and digital, to find the pronunciation and determine or clarify the precise meaning of key words and phrases.

L.5.5 Demonstrate understanding of figurative language, word relationships, and nuances in word meanings.
- ◆ L.5.5.A Interpret figurative language, including similes and metaphors, in context.
- ◆ L.5.5.B Recognize and explain the meaning of common idioms, adages, and proverbs.
- ◆ L.5.5.C Use the relationship between particular words (e.g., synonyms, antonyms, homographs) to better understand each of the words.

L.5.6 Acquire and use accurately grade-appropriate general academic and domain-specific words and phrases, including those that signal contrast, addition, and other logical relationships (e.g., *however, although, nevertheless, similarly, moreover, in addition*).

Table 2.1B

Sample Fifth-Grade Curriculum Map for English Language Arts (Reading: Literature)

Literary Text Type / Literature Standards	Realistic fiction	Biographies and autobiographies	Adventure stories	Narrative poem, limerick, and free verse poem	Folktales, legends, fables, fantasies, and myths	Staged plays
	RL.5.2 Theme of a story	RL.5.2 Theme of a story	RL.5.2 Theme of a story	RL.5.2 Theme of a poem	RL.5.2 Theme of a poem	RL.5.2 Theme of a drama
	RL.5.3 Compare and contrast characters, settings, or events in a story	RL.5.5 Chapters of a story	RL.5.5 Chapters of a story	RL.5.5 Stanzas of a poem	RL.5.3 Compare and contrast characters, settings, or events in a poem	RL.5.3 Compare and contrast characters, settings, or events in a drama
	RL.5.5 Chapters of a story	RL.5.6 Narrator's or speaker's point of view in a story	RL.5.6 Narrator's or speaker's point of view in a story	RL.5.7 Analyze how visual and multimedia elements contribute to a text	RL.5.7 Analyze how visual and multimedia elements contribute to a text	RL.5.5 Scenes of a drama
	RL.5.6 Narrator's or speaker's point of view in a story	RL.5.9 Compare and contrast stories in the same genre	RL.5.9 Compare and contrast stories in the same genre			RL.5.6 Narrator's or speaker's point of view in a drama

Table 2.1B, continued

Literary Text Type	Realistic fiction	Biographies and autobiographies	Adventure stories	Narrative poem, limerick, and free verse poem	Folktales, legends, fables, fantasies, and myths	Staged plays
Literature Standards, *continued*	RL.5.7 Analyze how visual and multimedia elements contribute to a text				L.5.9 Compare and contrast stories in the same genre	R.L.5.7 Analyze how visual and multimedia elements contribute to a text

Table 2.1C
Sample Fifth-Grade Curriculum Map for English Language Arts (Reading: Informational Text)

Literary Text Type	Realistic fiction	Biographies and autobiographies	Adventure stories	Narrative poem, limerick, and free verse poem	Folktales, legends, fables, fantasies, and myths	Staged plays
Informational Text Standards	RI.5.2 Determine two or more main ideas; summarize the text RI.5.3 Explain the relationships or interactions between two or more individuals, events, ideas, or concepts	RI.5.1 Quote accurately from a text when drawing inferences RI.5.2 Determine two or more main ideas of a text and explain how they are supported by key details; summarize the text	RI.5.2 Determine two or more main ideas; summarize the text RI.5.6 Analyze multiple accounts of the same event		RI.5.6 Analyze multiple accounts of the same event RI.5.6 Analyze multiple accounts of the same event	

Table 2.1C, continued

Literary Text Type	Realistic fiction	Biographies and autobiographies	Adventure stories	Narrative poem, limerick, and free verse poem	Folktales, legends, fables, fantasies, and myths	Staged plays
Informational Text Standards, *continued*	RI.5.8 Explain how an author uses reasons and evidence to support particular points in a text RI.5.5 Compare and contrast of events, ideas, concepts, or information in two or more texts RI.5.6 Analyze multiple accounts of the same event	RI.5.3 Explain the relationships or interactions between two or more individuals, events, ideas, or concepts RI.5.4 Determine the meaning of general academic and domain-specific words and phrases in a text relevant to a grade level topic or subject area				

Table 2.1C, continued

Literary Text Type	Realistic fiction	Biographies and autobiographies	Adventure stories	Narrative poem, limerick, and free verse poem	Folktales, legends, fables, fantasies, and myths	Staged plays
Informational Text Standards, *continued*		RI.5.5 Compare and contrast of events, ideas, concepts, or information in two or more texts RI.5.6 Analyze multiple accounts of the same event RI.5.7 Draw on information from multiple print or digital sources RI.5.9 Integrate information from several texts				

Table 2.1D
*Sample Fifth-Grade Curriculum Map of Yearlong Skills
for English Language Arts (Language)*

L.5.1 Demonstrate command of the conventions of standard English grammar and usage when writing or speaking.
- L.5.1.A Explain the function of conjunctions, prepositions, and interjections in general and their function in sentences.
- L.5.1.B Form and use the perfect (e.g., *I had walked*; *I have walked*; *I will have walked*) verb tenses.
- L.5.1.C Use verb tense to convey various times, sequences, states, and conditions.
- L.5.1.D Recognize and correct inappropriate shifts in verb tense.
- L.5.1.E Use correlative conjunctions (e.g., *either/or*, *neither/nor*).

L.5.2 Demonstrate command of the conventions of standard English capitalization, punctuation, and spelling when writing.
- L.5.2.A Use punctuation to separate items in a series.
- L.5.2.B Use a comma to separate an introductory element from the rest of the sentence.
- L.5.2.C Use a comma to set off the words yes and no (e.g., *Yes, thank you*), to set off a tag question from the rest of the sentence (e.g., *It's true, isn't it?*), and to indicate direct address (e.g., *Is that you, Steve?*).
- L5.2.D Use underlining, quotation marks, or italics to indicate titles of works.
- L5.2.E Spell grade-appropriate words correctly, consulting references as needed.

L.5.3 Use knowledge of language and its conventions when writing, speaking, reading, or listening.
- L.5.3.A Expand, combine, and reduce sentences for meaning, reader/listener interest, and style.
- L.5.3.B Compare and contrast the varieties of English (e.g., *dialects, registers*) used in stories, dramas, or poems.

Table 2.1E
Sample Fifth–Grade Curriculum Map of English Language Arts (Writing)

Literary Text Type*	Realistic fiction	Biographies and autobiographies	Adventure stories	Narrative poem, limerick, and free verse poem	Folktales, legends, fables, fantasies, and myths	Staged plays
Writing	W.5.3 Write narratives W.5.3.A Orient the reader by establishing a situation and introducing a narrator and/or characters W.5.3.B Use narrative techniques	W.5.1 Write opinion pieces W.5.1.A Introduce a topic, state an opinion, and create an organizational structure W.5.1.B Provide logically ordered reasons W.5.1.C Link opinion and reasons	W.5.3 Write narratives W.5.3.A Orient the reader by establishing a situation and introducing a narrator and/or characters W.5.3.B Use narrative techniques	W.5.2 Write informative or explanatory texts W.5.2.A Introduce a topic clearly, provide a general observation and focus, and group related information logically W.5.2.B Develop the topic with facts, definitions, concrete details, quotations, or other information	W.5.1 Write opinion pieces W.5.1.A Introduce a topic, state an opinion, and create an organizational structure W.5.1.B Provide logically ordered reasons W.5.1.C Link opinion and reasons	W.5.2 Write informative or explanatory texts W.5.2.A Introduce a topic clearly, provide a general observation and focus, and group related information logically

*These forms of writing are balanced throughout the year and could be integrated into other subject areas, including science, social studies, and mathematics.

Table 2.1E, continued

Literary Text Type*	Realistic fiction	Biographies and autobiographies	Adventure stories	Narrative poem, limerick, and free verse poem	Folktales, legends, fables, fantasies, and myths	Staged plays
Writing, *continued*	W.5.3.C Use a variety of transitional words, phrases, and clauses to manage the sequence of events W.5.3.D Use concrete words and phrases and sensory details to convey experiences and events precisely	W.5.1.D Provide a concluding statement or section related to the opinion presented	W.5.3.C Use a variety of transitional words, phrases, and clauses to manage the sequence of events W.5.3.D Use concrete words and phrases and sensory details to convey experiences and events precisely	W.5.2.C Link ideas within and across categories of information W.5.2.D Use precise language and domain-specific vocabulary W.5.2.E Provide a concluding statement or section related to the information or explanation presented	W.5.1.D Provide a concluding statement or section related to the opinion presented	W.5.2.B Develop the topic with facts, definitions, concrete details, quotations, or other information W.5.2.C Link ideas within and across categories of information W.5.2.D Use precise language and domain-specific vocabulary

Table 2.1E, continued

Literary Text Type*	Realistic fiction	Biographies and autobiographies	Adventure stories	Narrative poem, limerick, and free verse poem	Folktales, legends, fables, fantasies, and myths	Staged plays
Writing, *continued*	W.5.3.E Provide a conclusion that follows from the narrated experiences or events		W.5.3.E Provide a conclusion that follows from the narrated experiences or events			W.5.2.E Provide a concluding statement or section related to the information or explanation presented

Table 2.1F

Sample Fifth-Grade Curriculum Map of English Language Arts (Speaking and Listening)

Literary Text Type	Realistic fiction	Biographies and autobiographies	Adventure stories	Narrative poem, limerick, and free verse poem	Folktales, legends, fables, fantasies, and myths	Staged plays
Speaking and Listening	SL.5.2 Summarize a written text read aloud or information presented in diverse media and formats	SL.5.1 Engage effectively in a range of collaborative discussions SL.5.1.A Come to discussions prepared SL.5.1.B Follow agreed-upon rules for discussions and carry out assigned roles SL.5.1.C Pose and respond to specific questions SL.5.1.D Review the key ideas expressed and draw conclusions	SL.5.5 Include multimedia components and visual displays in presentations	SL.5.4 Report on a topic or text or present an opinion	SL.5.3 Summarize the points a speaker makes and explain how each claim is supported by reasons and evidence	SL.5.6 Adapt speech to a variety of contexts and tasks

Table 2.2
C3 Framework for Social Studies State Standards (Grade 5)

Geography	Native Americans	Economics	Colonization and Settlement	American Revolution	United States Constitution
Geographic Representations: Spatial Views of the World D2.Geo.1.3-5 D2.Geo.2.3-5 D2.Geo.3.3-5	Change, Continuity, and Context D2.His.1.3-5 D2.His.3.3-5 D2.His.5.3-5 D2.His.6.3-5	Economic Decision Making D2.Eco.1.3-5 D2.Eco.2.3-5	Change, Continuity, and Context D2.His.1.3-5 D2.His.2.3-5 D2.His.3.3-5 Perspectives D2.His.4.3-5 D2.His.5.3-5 D2.His.6.3-5	Change, Continuity, and Context D2.His.1.3-5 D2.His.2.3-5 D2.His.3.3-5 Perspectives D2.His.4.3-5 D2.His.5.3-5 D2.His.6.3-5	Civic and Political Institutions D2.Civ.1.3-5 D2.Civ.2.3-5 D2.Civ.3.3-5 D2.Civ.4.3-5 D2.Civ.5.3-5 D2.Civ.6.3-5
Human-Environment Interaction: Place, Regions, and Culture D2.Geo.4.3-5 D2.Geo.5.3-5 D2.Geo.6.3-5	Historical Sources and Evidence D2.His.9.3-5 D2.His.10.3-5 D2.His.12.3-5 D2.His.13.3-5	Exchange and Markets D2.Eco.3.3-5 D2.Eco.4.3-5 D2.Eco.5.3-5 D2.Eco.6.3-5 D2.Eco.7.3-5 D2.Eco.8.3-5 D2.Eco.9.3-5	Historical Sources and Evidence D2.His.9.3-5 D2.His.10.3-5 D2.His.11.3-5 D2.His.12.3-5 D2.His.13.3-5	Historical Sources and Evidence D2.His.9.3-5 D2.His.10.3-5 D2.His.11.3-5 D2.His.12.3-5 D2.His.13.3-5	Participation and Deliberation: Applying Civic Virtues and Democratic Principles D2.Civ.7.3-5 D2.Civ.8.3-5 D2.Civ.9.3-5 D2.Civ.10.3-5

Table 2.2, continued

Geography	Native Americans	Economics	Colonization and Settlement	American Revolution	United States Constitution
Human Population: Spatial Patterns and Movements D2.Geo.7.3-5 D2.Geo.8.3-5 D2.Geo.9.3-5	Causation and Augmentation D2.His.14.3-5 D2.His.16.3-5 D2.His.17.3-5	The National Economy D2.Eco.10.3-5 D2.Eco.11.3-5 D2.Eco.12.3-5 D2.Eco.13.3-5	Causation and Augmentation D2.His.14.3-5 D2.His.16.3-5 D2.His.17.3-5	Causation and Augmentation D2.His.14.3-5. D2.His.16.3-5. D2.His.17.3-5.	Processes, Rules, and Laws D2.Civ.11.3-5 D2.Civ.12.3-5 D2.Civ.13.3-5 D2.Civ.14.3-5
Global Interconnections: Changing Spatial Patterns D2.Geo.10.3-5 D2.Geo.11.3-5 D2.Geo.12.3-5		The Global Economy D2.Eco.14.3-5 D2.Eco.15.3-5			
Time, Continuity, and Change	Culture	Time, Continuity, and Change	Culture	Time, Continuity, and Change	Time, Continuity, and Change
People, Places, and Environments	Time, Continuity, and Change	People, Places, and Environments	Time, Continuity, and Change	People, Places, and Environments	People, Places, and Environments
Individual Development and Identity *continued*	Individual Development and Identity *continued*	Individual Development and Identity *continued*	People, Places, and Environments *continued*	Individual Development and Identity *continued*	Environments *continued*

Table 2.2, continued

Geography	Native Americans	Economics	Colonization and Settlement	American Revolution	United States Constitution
	Individuals, Groups, and Institutions	Production, Distribution, and Consumption	Individual Development and Identity	Individuals, Groups, and Institutions	Individual Development and Identity
	Power, Authority, and Governance	Global Connections	Individuals, Groups, and Institutions	Power, Authority, and Governance	Individuals, Groups, and Institutions
	Science, Technology, and Society		Power, Authority, and Governance	Science, Technology, and Society	Power, Authority, and Governance
	Global Connections		Science, Technology, and Society	Global Connections	Production, Distribution, and Consumption
	Civic Ideals and Practices		Global Connections	Civic Ideals and Practices	Civic Ideals and Practices
			Civic Ideals and Practices		

1. **Culture:** Learning how human beings create, learn, share, and adapt to mold their lives and society.
2. **Time, Continuity, and Change:** Learning about the past through studying values and beliefs while learning how history formed the current world through skill acquisition, inquiry, and understanding.
3. **People, Places, and Environments:** Learning various aspects of people and places in addition to growing in understanding spatial skills and new perspectives of the world.
4. **Individual Development and Identity:** Learning self-awareness and development through the influences of family, peers, and formal institutions.
5. **Individuals, Groups, and Institutions:** Learning the influences of families, education, government structures, and organized religion institutions.
6. **Power, Authority, and Governance:** Learning the roles of power, authority, and governmental structure through examination between democratic and nondemocratic political systems.
7. **Production, Distribution, and Consumption:** Learning how domestic and global economic topics impact how citizens prepare for production, distribution, and consumption of goods and services.
8. **Science, Technology, and Society:** Learning the importance of the relationships among science, technology, and society while understanding past and present advances in science and technology.
9. **Global Connections:** Learning how globalization enhances interdependence and requires an understanding of global connections among world societies.
10. **Civic Ideals and Practices:** Learning the importance of democracy and active citizenship with critical attention to full participation in society.

The bottom row of Table 2.2 displays how each of the six social studies topics in the table can be tied to C3 Framework themes in a fifth-grade concept-based unit. Social studies can be an excellent place to begin and make natural connections to other curricular topics.

Science

The Next Generation Science Standards contain four major units of study. These are mapped out in Tables 2.3A–2.3E and include process science standards in addition to the content standards for the fifth-grade level. These also include crosscutting standards (National Research Council, 2012), the applica-

Table 2.3A

Next Generation Science Standards (Grade 5)

	Matter and Energy in Organisms and Ecosystems	Structure and Properties of Matter	Earth's Systems	Space Systems: Stars and the Solar System
Next Generation Science Standards	5-PS3-1. Use models to describe that energy in animals' food (used for body repair, growth, motion, and to maintain body warmth) was once energy from the sun. 5-LS1-1. Support an argument that plants get the materials they need for growth chiefly from air and water. 5-LS2-1. Develop a model to describe the movement of matter among plants, animals, decomposers, and the environment.	5-PS1-1. Develop a model to describe that matter is made of particles too small to be seen. 5-PS1-2. Measure and graph quantities to provide evidence that regardless of the type of change that occurs when heating, cooling, or mixing substances, the total weight of matter is conserved. 5-PS1-3. Make observations and measurements to iden- tify materials based on their properties.	5-ESS2-1. Develop a model using an example to describe ways the geosphere, bio- sphere, hydrosphere, and/or atmosphere interact. 5-ESS2-2. Describe and graph the amounts of salt water and fresh water in various reservoirs to provide evidence about the distribu- tion of water on Earth. 5-ESS3-1. Obtain and combine information about ways individual communities use science ideas to protect the Earth's resources and environment.	5-PS2-1. Support an argu- ment that the gravitational force exerted by Earth on objects is directed down. 5-ESS1-1. Support an argument that differences in the apparent brightness of the sun compared to other stars is due to their relative distances from Earth.

Table 2.3A, continued

Next Generation Science Standards, *continued*	5-PS1-4. Conduct an investigation to determine whether the mixing of two or more substances results in new substances.	5-ESS1-2. Represent data in graphical displays to reveal patterns of daily changes in length and direction of shadows, day and night, and the seasonal appearance of some stars in the night sky.

Table 2.3B

Next Generation Science Standards—Science and Engineering Domain (Grade 5)

	Matter and Energy in Organisms and Ecosystems	Structure and Properties of Matter	Earth's Systems	Space Systems: Stars and the Solar System
Science and Engineering Practices	Developing and Using Models (5-PS3-1, 5-LS2-1) Engaging in Argument from Evidence (5-LS1-1) Science Models, Laws, Mechanisms, and Theories Explain Natural Phenomena (5-LS2-1)	Developing and Using Models (5-PS1-1) Planning and Carrying Out Investigations (5-PS1-3, 5-PS1-4) Using Mathematics and Computational Thinking (5-PS1-2)	Developing and Using Models (5-ESS2-1) Using Mathematics and Computational Thinking (5-ESS2-2) Obtaining, Evaluating, and Communicating Information (5-ESS3-1)	Analyzing and Interpreting Data (5-ESS1-2) Engaging in Argument from Evidence (5-PS2-1, 5-ESS1-1)
Disciplinary Core Ideas	PS3.D: Energy in Chemical Processes and Everyday Life (5-PS3-1) LS1.C: Organization for Matter and Energy Flow in Organisms (secondary to 5-PS3-1, 5-LS1-1) LS2.A: Interdependent Relationships in Ecosystems (5-LS2-1) LS2.B: Cycles of Matter and Energy Transfer in Ecosystems (5-LS2-1)	PS1.A: Structure and Properties of Matter (5-PS1-2, 5-PS1-3, 5-PS1-4) PS1.B: Chemical Reactions (5-PS1-2, 5-PS1-4)	ESS2.A: Earth Materials and Systems (5-ESS2-1) ESS2.C: The Roles of Water in Earth's Surface Processes (5-ESS2-2) ESS3.C: Human Impacts on Earth Systems (5-ESS3-1)	PS2.B: Types of Interactions ESS1.A: The Universe and its Stars ESS1.B: Earth and the Solar System (5-ESS1-2)

Table 2.3C

Next Generation Science Standards—Crosscutting Concepts (Grade 5)

	Matter and Energy in Organisms and Ecosystems	Structure and Properties of Matter	Earth's Systems	Space Systems: Stars and the Solar System
Crosscutting Concepts	Systems and System Models (5-LS2-1) Energy and Matter (5-LS1-1, 5-PS3-1)	Cause and Effect (5-PS1-4) Scale, Proportion, and Quantity (5-PS1-1, 5-PS1-2, 5-PS1-3) Scientific Knowledge Assumes an Order and Consistency in Natural Systems (5-PS1-2)	Scale, Proportion, and Quantity (5-ESS2-2) Systems and System Models (5-ESS2-1, 5-ESS3-1) Science Addresses Questions About the Natural and Material World (5-ESS3-1)	Patterns (5-ESS1-2) Cause and Effect (5-PS2-1) Scale, Proportion, and Quantity (5-ESS1-1)

Table 2.3D

Next Generation Science Standards—CCSS Connections for English Language Arts (Grade 5)

	Matter and Energy in Organisms and Ecosystems	Structure and Properties of Matter	Earth's Systems	Space Systems: Stars and the Solar System
CCSS Connections (ELA)	RI.5.1 Quote accurately from a text when explaining what the text says explicitly and when drawing inferences from the text. (5-LS1-1) RI.5.7 Draw on information from multiple print or digital sources, demonstrating the ability to locate an answer to a question quickly or to solve a problem efficiently. (5-PS3-1, 5-LS2-1) RI.5.9 Integrate information from several texts on the same topic in order to write or speak about the subject knowledgeably. (5-LS1-1)	RI.5.7 Draw on information from multiple print or digital sources. (5-PS1-1) W.5.7 Conduct short research projects that use several sources to build knowledge through investigation of different aspects of a topic. (5-PS1-2, 5-PS1-3, 5-PS1-4) W.5.8 Recall relevant information from experiences or gather relevant information from print and digital sources; summarize or paraphrase information in notes and finished work, and provide a list of sources. (5-PS1-2, 5-PS1-3, 5-PS1-4)	RI.5.1 Quote accurately from a text when explaining what the text says explicitly and when drawing inferences from the text. (5-ESS3-1) RI.5.7 Draw on information from multiple print or digital sources, demonstrating the ability to locate an answer to a question quickly or to solve a problem efficiently. (5-ESS2-1, 5-ESS2-2, 5-ESS3-1) RI.5.9 Integrate information from several texts on the same topic in order to write or speak about the subject knowledgeably. (5-ESS3-1)	RI.5.1 Quote accurately from a text when explaining what the text says explicitly and when drawing inferences from the text. (5-PS2-1, 5-ESS1-1) RI.5.7 Draw on information from multiple print or digital sources, demonstrating the ability to locate an answer to a question quickly or to solve a problem efficiently. (5-ESS1-1) RI.5.8 Explain how an author uses reasons and evidence to support particular points in a text, identifying which reasons and evidence support which point(s). (5-ESS1-1)

Table 2.3D, continued

	Matter and Energy in Organisms and Ecosystems	Structure and Properties of Matter	Earth's Systems	Space Systems: Stars and the Solar System
CCSS Connections (ELA), *continued*	W.5.1 Write opinion pieces on topics or texts, supporting a point of view with reasons and information. (5-LS1-1) SL.5.5 Include multimedia components (e.g., graphics, sound) and visual displays in presentations when appropriate to enhance the development of main ideas or themes. (5-PS3-1, 5-LS2-1)	W.5.9 Draw evidence from literary or informational texts to support analysis, reflection, and research. (5-PS1-2, 5-PS1-3, 5-PS1-4)	W.5.8 Recall relevant information from experiences or gather relevant information from print and digital sources; summarize or paraphrase information in notes and finished work and provide a list of sources. (5-ESS2-2, 5-ESS3-1) W.5.9 Draw evidence from literary or informational texts to support analysis, reflection, and research. (5-ESS3-1) SL.5.5 Include multimedia and visual displays in presentations when appropriate to enhance the development of main ideas or themes. (5-ESS2-1, 5-ESS2-2)	RI.5.9 Integrate information from several texts on the same topic in order to write or speak about the subject knowledgeably. (5-PS2-1, 5-ESS1-1) W.5.1 Write opinion pieces on topics or texts, supporting a point of view with reasons and information. (5-PS2-1, 5-ESS1-1) SL 5.5 Include multimedia components (e.g., graphics, sound) and visual displays in presentations when appropriate to enhance the development of main ideas or themes. (5-ESS1-2)

Table 2.3E

Next Generation Science Standards—CCSS Connections for Mathematics (Grade 5)

	Matter and Energy in Organisms and Ecosystems	Structure and Properties of Matter	Earth's Systems	Space Systems: Stars and the Solar System
CCSS Connections (Mathematics)	MP2 Reason abstractly and quantitatively. (5-LS1-1, 5-LS2-1) MP4 Model with mathematics. (5-LS1-1, 5-LS2-1) MP5 Use appropriate tools strategically. (5-LS1-1)	MP2 Reason abstractly and quantitatively. (5-PS1-1, 5-PS1-2, 5-PS1-3) MP4 Model with mathematics. (5-PS1-1, 5-PS1-2, 5-PS1-3) MP5 Use appropriate tools strategically. (5-PS1-2, 5-PS1-3)	MP2 Reason abstractly and quantitatively. (5-ESS2-1, 5-ESS2-2, 5-ESS3-1) MP4 Model with mathematics. (5-ESS2-1, 5-ESS2-2, 5-ESS3-1)	MP2 Reason abstractly and quantitatively. (5-ESS1-1, 5-ESS1-2) MP4 Model with mathematics. (5-ESS1-1, 5-ESS1-2) 5.NBT.A.2 Explain patterns in the number of zeros of the product when multiplying and use whole-number exponents. (5-ESS1-1)

Table 2.3E, continued

	Matter and Energy in Organisms and Ecosystems	Structure and Properties of Matter	Earth's Systems	Space Systems: Stars and the Solar System
CCSS Connections (Mathematics), *continued*	5.MD.A.1 Convert among different-sized standard measurement units within a given measurement system (e.g., convert 5 cm to 0.05 m), and use these conversions in solving multi-step, real world problems. (5–LS1–1)	5.NBT.A.2 Explain patterns in the number of zeros of the product when multiplying a number by powers of 10, and explain patterns in the placement of the decimal point when a decimal is multiplied or divided by a power of 10. Use whole-number exponents to denote powers of 10. 5.NF.B.7 Apply and extend previous understandings of division to divide unit fractions by whole numbers and whole numbers by unit fractions. (5–PS1–1)	5.G.A.2 Represent real world and mathematical problems by graphing points in the first quadrant of the coordinate plane, and interpret coordinate values of points in the context of the situation. (5–ESS2–1)	5.G.A.2 Represent real world and mathematical problems by graphing points in the first quadrant of the coordinate plane, and interpret coordinate values of points in the context of the situation. (5–ESS1–2)

51

Table 2.3E, continued

	Matter and Energy in Organisms and Ecosystems	Structure and Properties of Matter	Earth's Systems	Space Systems: Stars and the Solar System
CCSS Connections (Mathematics), *continued*		5.MD.A.1 Convert among different-sized standard measurement units within a given measurement system (e.g., convert 5 cm to 0.05 m), and use these conversions in solving multi-step, real world problems. (5-PS1-2) 5.MD.C.3 Recognize volume as an attribute of solid figures and understand concepts of volume measurement. (5-PS1-1) 5.MD.C.4 Measure volumes by counting, using cubic cm, cubic in, cubic ft. and improvised units. (5-PS1-1)		

tion of the CCSS for English language arts, and mathematics indicators. The standards are included in Tables 2.3D and 2.3E to outline natural connections to language arts and mathematics. These relationships support the integration of the skills into the concepts. Educators, who have a naturally sequential way of organizing curriculum, will save the time and energy usually required for brainstorming ideas by adding these skills into a predominantly content-emphasized discipline. Forming cross-curricular ties will assist the thematic and broad-based concepts created later in the process.

Mathematics

Incorporating mathematics in a concept-based unit can be a challenge. Good mathematics instruction builds upon previously learned concepts and skills with a continuing spiral. As noted in the science units, integrated English language arts and mathematics standards work at an application level. Mathematics has some natural possibilities related to science. There are a couple of domains of mathematics that may be separated from daily and progressive math instruction. For instance, data analysis and measurement skills go well with science. Care will need to be taken in making sure that students have experience with reading scales and are able to manipulate numbers in decimal or fractional form. Students graph and interpret data, measure length and capacity, and track information and times. It is also important to map out mathematics skills in tandem or ahead of the application of the skills in science units. Age and grade development should also be considered in terms of what mathematical operations (add, subtract, multiply, or divide) students are able to do. An alternative might be the appropriate use of a calculator to perform the operation. An example of this implementation would be understanding the concepts of all four operations but not how to manipulate numbers in a decimal format. The same idea would be true of the necessary English language arts skills. Examples would be limited attention to spelling, punctuation, and grammar usage.

Curriculum Mapping and Differentiation

A curriculum map can be the foundation for differentiating instruction. Tomlinson (1999) made the following connection regarding the importance of curriculum mapping before a teacher can begin to differentiate instruction:

The first step in making differentiation work is the hardest. In fact, the same first step is required to make all teaching and learning effective: We have to know where we want to end up before we start out—and plan to get there. That is, we must have solid curriculum and instruction in place before we differentiate them. That's harder than it seems. (p. 12)

Once the teacher knows where he or she is headed through the mapping process, anticipating what differentiation may be needed becomes clearer. An overview of skills, and possibly previous experience, helps a teacher to predict what skills students may have as a solid academic base for adding new learning. This overview also helps provide natural advancement and indicate where enrichment or acceleration may need to be available. Differentiation is grounded in assessment, and it would not be unique in a concept-based instructional classroom. When reviewing a curricular map from a vertical perspective, looking at the grades above and below, a teacher has a better notion of what students have learned and where they will be headed in future grade levels. Looking back helps both teacher and student know what gaps there may be in a student's educational past. Even though a curriculum map is intended to communicate learning experiences for a particular grade level, gaps in learning and misconceptions can still occur. When seeking to go beyond the basic grade-level standard, teachers can consider their school or district's practices when providing learning opportunities. Is it a deeper thinking enrichment model, or are students accelerated to the next grade level?

Curriculum mapping outlines the generalizations, facts, and terms that are important for students to learn. These would be closely tied to the academic standards. As a unit of study is being developed, a teacher or curriculum committee can create highly engaging learning experiences knowing what the specific learning goals are. Mapping allows teachers to push students a little out of their comfort zones yet meet them where they are, make connections to the real world, and tie evidence of learning to these expected outcomes.

Chapter 3

Creating Rich Learning Experiences, Transfers, and Applications

As introduced in Chapter 1, Erickson is the leading expert on the topic of concept-based teaching and unit development. She has presented at international educational conferences and worked with schools all over the world. Much of her work is related to the International Baccalaureate program. This approach to curriculum is much deeper than what Erickson (2012) called a two-dimensional model of skills and facts. She promoted a three-dimensional model of deeper thinking by students who are expected to understand principles and make generalizations of concepts that are supported by cognitive and learning research:

> Three-dimensional models focus on concepts, principles and generalizations, using related facts and skills as tools to gain deeper understanding of disciplinary content, transdisciplinary themes and interdisciplinary issues, and to facilitate conceptual transfer through time, across cultures and across situations. Three-dimensional models value a solid base of critical factual knowledge across the disciplines, but they raise the bar for curriculum and instruction by shifting the design focus to the conceptual level of understanding. This focus necessarily requires a supporting role for factual knowledge. (p. 4)

DOI:10.4324/9781003233770-5

Concept-Based Instruction

Teachers often set lesson objectives with a focus on what students should know and be able to do. Examples of knowledge include:

- ◆ the phases of the life cycle of a butterfly,
- ◆ 4 times 5 equals 20,
- ◆ Christopher Columbus is given credit for discovering America in 1492, or
- ◆ a silent "e" at the end of a word usually makes the vowel sound long.

Skills would include:

- ◆ accurately solving a long division problem,
- ◆ correctly editing a sentence with the correct capitalization and punctuation,
- ◆ creating a model of the solar system, or
- ◆ tracing events leading to the American Revolution.

Concept-based teaching deliberately specifies that students understand and transfer knowledge to a novel situation. The curriculum unit has a constructivist framework, beginning with the whole and expanding into parts. Students often collaborate with others and frequently use primary sources of information. The classroom teacher is more of an orchestrator and facilitator as opposed to the dispenser of the information. Although the instructor has a plan, there must also be opportunities for students to find answers to their own questions and interests. This results in deeper learning. Erickson et al. (2017) outlined the elements of a concept-based unit as follows:

> **Fact:** A statement of truth.
> **Topic:** A category of study with a body of related facts to be learned.
> **Concept:** An organizing idea, represented by one or two words. Examples have common attributes.
> **Principle:** A form of generalization but is a truth that holds consistently through time.
> **Generalization:** Connection/relatedness of two or more concepts. (pp. 33–34)

The next step in developing a concept-based unit is to review the curriculum maps and look at broad-based themes. Table 3.1 is a list of themes that can have the potential to tie individual subject areas together. This is not a complete list, but many of these themes can fit very well. As students go through the various grade levels, they first learn that a noun is a person, place, or thing. A little later, they learn that a noun can also be an idea, which is a more abstract concept.

Table 3.1
Concept-Based Unit Themes

Adaptation	Creation	Immigration	Population
Aesthetics	Culture	Interaction	Power
Augmentation	Diversity	Interdependence	Principles
Beauty	Empathy	Justice	Relationships
Beliefs	Environment	Leadership	Revolution
Change	Ethics	Migration	Rights
Communications	Evolution	Movement	Social Roles
Community	Exploration	Normalcy	Structure
Conflict	Expression	Order	Survival
Context	Extinction	Origins	Symbolism
Continuity	Function	Patterns	Systems
Cooperation	Honor	Perception	Traditions
Courage	Identity	Perspective	Values

Examples of abstract nouns would include *beauty*, *power*, *heritage*, *integrity*, and others. Nonexamples would include *Thanksgiving* (or any other holiday), *monsters*, *apples*, or *chemical compounds*. These abstract nouns are like the concepts or "big ideas" that might be chosen; they are usually not tangible or visible.

By revisiting the fifth-grade example of a curriculum map in Chapter 2, one can now look at the topics and consider themes across each of the six units. The Lexile Framework for Reading (https://lexile.com) is a good resource for finding books for a topic of study. In Table 3.2, the website was used to look for possible matching books of the genre of each unit. A layer of differentiation was added based on the website recommendation of three levels of texts according to the grade level. Each book option matches the Lexile range within each genre. There is also a crossover of the three ranges that can allow teachers to be flexible in grouping students. For example, a student who reads at a higher Lexile level may still have trouble with a specific reading comprehension skill, such as drawing conclusions or summarizing. The teacher could group students with like academic needs for an intervening lesson on that skill and then ask them to apply it in some way using the text at their Lexile level. Many of the literature and informational standards may be taught through these various genres. The informational text standards may be better applied and mastered through the content areas of science and social studies.

Table 3.3 presents a year of fifth-grade language arts units, with each unit lasting 6 weeks. The curriculum map reveals the major genres of literature found in the standards. These are listed at the top of the six columns of the chart. Each row identifies an element of language arts (literature, informational text, writing,

Table 3.2

Literacy Genres With Potential Texts by Lexile and Fountas & Pinnell Levels (Grade 5)

Lexile (Fountas & Pinnell Levels)	Realistic fiction	Biographies and autobiographies (potential for self-selected research)	Adventure stories	Narrative poem, limerick, and free verse poem	Folktales, legends, fables, fantasies, and myths	Staged plays
330–810L (J–S)	Because of Mr. Terupt (Rob Buyea), Superfudge (Judy Blume), The Face on the Milk Carton (Caroline B. Cooney)	Abraham Lincoln: The Great Emancipator (Augusta Stevenson), Who Was Amelia Earhart? (Kate Boehm Jerome), Who Was Daniel Boone? (Sydelle Kramer)	Danger on Midnight River (Gary Paulsen), Small as an Elephant (Jennifer Richard Jacobson), Flight of the Phoenix (R. L. LaFevers)	Hoops (Robert Burleigh), Come With Me: Poems for a Journey (Naomi Shihab Nye), No More Homework! No More Tests!: Kids' Favorite Funny School Poems (Giggle Poetry) (Bruce Lansky)	The Adventures of Robin Hood (Howard Pyle), Scary Stories to Tell in the Dark (Alvin Schwartz), Nice Shot, Cupid! (Kate McMullan), Heroes, Gods, and Monsters of the Greek Myths (Bernard Evslin)	Harry Potter and the Cursed Child, Parts One and Two (J. K. Rowling, John Tiffany, and Jack Thorne), Plays Magazine (drama magazine for kids)

Table 3.2, continued

Lexile *(Fountas & Pinnell Levels)*	Realistic fiction	Biographies and autobiographies (potential for self-selected research)	Adventure stories	Narrative poem, limerick, and free verse poem	Folktales, legends, fables, fantasies, and myths	Staged plays
610–1050L (O–Z)	*Bud, Not Buddy* (Christopher Paul Curtis), *The Best School Year Ever* (Barbara Robinson), *A Dog's Purpose* (W. Bruce Cameron)	*Who Was Albert Einstein?* (Jess Brallier), *Thomas Edison (10 Days)* (David Colbert), *Abraham Lincoln: Friend of the People* (Clara Ingram Judson), *My Side of the Mountain* (Jean Craighead George)	*Dogsong* (Gary Paulsen), *Inside Out and Back Again* (Thanhha Lai), *Wild Life* (Cynthia DeFelice)	*Love That Dog* (Sharon Creech), *Come With Me: Poems for a Journey* (Naomi Shihab Nye), *No More Homework! No More Tests! Kids' Favorite Funny School Poems* (Giggle Poetry) (Bruce Lansky), *Recess, Rhyme, and Reason: A Collection of Poems About School* (Patricia M. Stockland)	*The Adventures of Robin Hood* (Howard Pyle), *American Tall Tales* (Adrien Stoutenburg), *Two Old Women* (Velma Wallis), *The Green Man: Tales From the Mythic Forest* (Ellen Datlow), *Heroes, Gods, and Monsters of the Greek Myths* (Bernard Evslin)	

Table 3.2, continued

Lexile *(Fountas & Pinnell Levels)*	Realistic fiction	Biographies and autobiographies (potential for self-selected research)	Adventure stories	Narrative poem, limerick, and free verse poem	Folktales, legends, fables, fantasies, and myths	Staged plays
880–1050L (U–Z)	*The Misfits* (James Howe), *Safe at Home* (Mike Lupica), *The Higher Power of Lucky* (Susan Patron)	*J. R. R. Tolkien (Writers Uncovered)* (Vic Parker), *Lost Boy, Lost Girl: Escaping Civil War in Sudan* (John Bul Dau and Martha Arual Akech), *My Side of the Mountain* (Jean Craighead George)	*Hatchet* (Gary Paulsen), *The Blue Sword* (Robin McKinley), *William S. and the Great Escape* (Zilpha Keatley Snyder)	*Love That Dog* (Sharon Creech), *Recess, Rhyme, and Reason: A Collection of Poems About School* (Patricia M. Stockland), *Living Up the Street* (Gary Soto)	*American Tall Tales* (Adrien Stoutenburg), *Cut From the Same Cloth: American Women of Myth, Legend, and Tall Tale* (Robert D. San Souci), *Two Old Women* (Velma Wallis), *The Green Man: Tales From the Mythic Forest* (Ellen Datlow), *D'Aulaire's Book of Greek Myths* (Ingri and Edgar Parin d'Aulaire)	

Table 3.3

CCSS for ELA Mapped Out by Grade Level and Genre (Grade 5)

	Realistic fiction	Biographies and autobiographies (potential for self-selected research)	Adventure stories	Narrative poem, limerick, and free verse poem	Folktales, legends, fables, fantasies, and myths	Staged plays
Literature	RL.5.1 RL.5.5 RL.5.2 RL.5.6 RL.5.3 RL.5.7	RL.5.1 RL.5.6 RL.5.2 RL.5.9 RL.5.5	RL.5.1 RL.5.2 RL.5.5 RL.5.6 RL.5.9	RL.5.1 RL.5.2 RL.5.5 RL.5.7	RL.5.1 RL.5.7 RL.5.2 RL.5.9 RL.5.3	RL.5.1 RL.5.5 RL.5.2 RL.5.6 RL.5.3 RL.5.7
Informational Text	RI.5.2 RI.5.5 RI.5.6	RI.5.1 RI.5.6 RI.5.2 RI.5.7 RI.5.3 RI.5.8 RI.5.4 RI.5.9 RI.5.5	RI.5.2 RI.5.6		RI.5.6	
Writing	W.5.3	W.5.1	W.5	W.5.2	W.5.1	W.5.2
Speaking and Listening	SL.5.2	SL.5.1	SL.5.5	SL.5.4	SL.5.3	SL.5.6

and speaking and listening). The intersection of the columns and rows matches up the standards emphasized during a 6-week unit experience. Attention was given to ensure that these skills were not placed in a "one and done" format that does not allow for an opportunity to repeat or refine previously taught curriculum, except for speaking and listening skills. (This curriculum map happened to include speaking and listening skills in this format with the assumption that they are not considered to be of as high importance as the others.) Regardless, teachers may certainly continue to look for ways to include these skills when natural and appropriate across disciplines. An example would be classroom presentations in which students share information orally.

The opposite was true of writing skills in this example. Repeating writing kept it as a power skill, an assumption based on achievement data or the curriculum mapping team's decision. Laying out the curriculum standards throughout the year is the science of teaching—creating the objectives for the lessons. The teacher is ready to execute these objectives through artful decisions made in creating meaningful engagement, deep thinking, and integrated units of study.

Similar to Table 3.3, Table 3.4 identifies six social studies topics that emerged through the mapping process. As stated in Chapter 2, humanities seem to be an easy discipline to begin with. People often think of history and particular time periods when it comes to social studies, but the social studies standards communicate that economics, geography, and government are also major topics within the discipline. Sometimes, an equal number of topics may not occur in all subject areas. Just four main topics emerged in science with many standards and content. Notice how these are placed to cross over one-and-one-half of the social studies topics. In this way, the concept drives the unit, with the topics and standards falling in place with the opportunity to learn content from multiple conceptual perspectives. It could be difficult to juggle, but theoretically a teacher could decide on six themes with more units of study. Remember that thematic concepts are universal. Some subjects and topics are just natural fits to those conceptual themes.

The column on the left side of Table 3.4 includes the science and English language arts standards. This arrangement has two purposes. The first is to identify the standards needing instruction in each of the science topics. The second is to reemphasize the English language arts standards identified in the NCSS. The bottom row demonstrates the importance of communication skills in other subject areas. Again, the goal of a concept-based unit is to break down the individual subject areas and build deep and rich connections at a higher thinking level and from different perspectives.

Note that mathematics has not been mapped out based on topic, but the science map could be greatly influenced by the logical and progressive sequence of the core mathematics curriculum. If mathematics were to be mapped out, just

Table 3.4

Yearlong Curriculum Map of Science and Social Studies With English Language Arts and Mathematics Connections

Social Studies	Geography	Native Americans	Economics	Colonization and Settlement	American Revolution	U.S. Constitution
Science Disciplinary Core Ideas	**Matter and Energy in Organisms and Ecosystems:** PS3.D (5-PS3-1) LS1.C (secondary to 5-PS3-1, 5-LS1-1) LS2.A (5-LS2-1) LS2.B (5-LS2-1)	**Structure and Properties of Matter:** PS1.A (5-PS1-1, 5-PS1-2, 5-PS1-3) PS1.B (5-PS1-2, 5-PS1-4)		**Earth's Systems:** ESS2.A (5-ESS2-1) ESS2.C (5-ESS2-2) ESS3.C (5-ESS3-1)		**Space Systems: Stars and the Solar System:** PS2.B (5-PS2-1) ESS1.A (5-ESS1-1) ESS1.B (5-ESS1-2)
Common Core Standards Connections (ELA)	RI.5.1 (5-LS1-1) RI.5.7 (5-PS3-1, 5-LS2-1) RI.5.9 (5-LS1-1) W.5.1 (5-LS1-1)	RI.5.7 (5-PS1-1) W.5.7 (5-PS1-2, 5-PS1-3, 5-PS1-4) W.5.8 (5-PS1-2, 5-PS1-3, 5-PS1-4)		RI.5.1 (5-ESS3-1) RI.5.7 (5-ESS2-1, 5-ESS2-2, 5-ESS3-1) RI.5.9 (5-ESS3-1)		RI.5.1 (5-PS2-1, 5-ESS1-1) RI.5.7 (5-ESS1-1) RI.5.8 (5-ESS1-1)

Table 3.4, continued

Social Studies	Geography	Native Americans	Economics	Colonization and Settlement	American Revolution	U.S. Constitution
Common Core Standards Connections (ELA), *continued*	SL.5.5 (5-PS3-1, 5-LS2-1)	W.5.9 (5-PS1-2, 5-PS1-3, 5-PS1-4)		W.5.8 (5-ESS2-2, 5-ESS3-1) W.5.9 (5-ESS3-1) SL.5.5 (5-ESS2-1, 5-ESS2-2)		
Common Core Standards Connections (Mathematics)	MP2 (5-LS1-1, 5-LS2-1) MP4 (5-LS1-1, 5-LS2-1) MP5 (5-LS1-1) 5.MD.A.1 (5-LS1-1)	MP2 (5-PS1-1, 5-PS1-2, 5-PS1-3) MP4 (5-PS1-1, 5-PS1-2, 5-PS1-3) MP5 (5-PS1-2, 5-PS1-3) 5.NBT.A.1 (5-PS1-1) 5.NF.B.7 (5-PS1-1) 5.MD.A.1 (5-PS1-2)		MP2 (5-ESS2-1, 5-ESS2-2, 5-ESS3-1) MP4 (5-ESS2-1, 5-ESS2-2, 5-ESS3-1) 5.G.2 (5-ESS2-1)		

Table 3.4, continued

Social Studies	Geography	Native Americans	Economics	Colonization and Settlement	American Revolution	U.S. Constitution
Common Core Standards Connections (Mathematics), *continued*			5.MD.C.3 (5–PS1–1) 5.MD.C.4 (5–PS1–1)			

like the language arts standards, there should be an opportunity for students to have skills spiraled back for practice and to apply these skills in new situations.

Social Studies and Science Themes

As stated earlier, social studies is often the best place to look for broad-based concepts. Once these themes have been determined, the other disciplines in the section should be reviewed for having the same themes present. One thing to remember about concept-based unit development is the flexibility of subject matter because of the wide net of themes possible. Based on the curriculum mapping done in the beginning, the following summarizes the next steps:

1. Identify multiple potential themes after reviewing the social studies topics. Looking for multiple thematic possibilities will help to produce more natural topic choices in the other disciplines.

2. Begin assigning themes in other subject areas. Science is probably the next subject area to assign major themes.

3. Look for same-theme units of study in social studies and science. It may become necessary to move units to a different point in the year to align the themes correctly.

4. Repeat the process with literature and writing. It might become necessary to make some adjustments. The potential reading choices should be complementary to the concept theme. A word of caution: Do not confuse or blend the topics of science and social studies with the literature choices. The big goal of creating a concept-based unit is to provide multiple perspectives for generalizing. A common mistake is letting the social studies topic dictate the literature study. This can result in multiple historical fiction novels being the only genre that students experience. A good curriculum map should eliminate that problem.

5. If there is a desire to include mathematics, teachers should map out the units in a logical manner. In Table 3.4, for example, the teacher would plan whole-number multiplication and division at the beginning of the year, and multiplication and division of fractions and decimals during the second half of the year. It is assumed that the whole number operations are needed through most of the year for some of the science experiences, starting with Structure and Properties and Matter in relation to the CCSS connections.

6. The final step would be to include common ancillary classes, such as visual arts, physical education, and general music, in the concept unit. This is probably more logical at the elementary level. Because the sec-

ondary level offers a wider range of elective choices, it is usually best to stick to the core subjects that all students experience.

Cross-Curricular Connections

Taking the maps created in each discipline, now is the opportunity to look for common concept-based themes to tie the unit across the curriculum. In the previous section, the brainstorming of possible themes occurred. The list of potential themes is quite flexible and large in scope for social studies. Looking at the reduced list (see Table 3.5) makes it easier to continue this process for science, with the goal of focusing on the final six themes that these two subjects have in common. As presented in Table 3.4, the number of clear units in science is four instead of six. The decision needs to be made as to whether a unit might cross over two conceptual themes, alternate between the two subjects, or whether the four units will vary in length.

Table 3.6 demonstrates a cross-curricular connection of thematic concepts of science and social studies. Multiple themes are listed. The italicized theme is the one chosen for this unit. Choosing the final theme is really a matter of personal preference by the unit designer. This decision is often based on the perceived flexibility of the concept and how accessible generalizations and theories will be discovered based on the unit's goals and content.

Based on a 9-week grading period, it is necessary to have a balance of assessment and performance reports. In order to accomplish this, the social studies topics will be 6 weeks in length, and the science topics will be 9 weeks each.

In summary, the first unit will cover weeks 1–6 of the science topic; the second will occur over weeks 7–9 (the last 3 weeks of the first quarter) and all of the second quarter. The second semester would follow the same plan. It would begin with the third science topic taking place over the entire third quarter (weeks 19–27) and over the fourth and fifth conceptual themes. The fourth science unit would be taught over the last 9 weeks and cross over the remainder of the fifth theme and all of the last theme.

A teacher might have to make a couple of alignment decisions. Based on the example in Table 3.6, the economics topic has the least amount of thematic crossover with other topics. It can continue to be a stand-alone topic, or it can be integrated into the other topics, resulting in five themes rather than six. Geography could be a second topic taught in this manner. By creating the units in this way, four units would be produced. Again, a word of caution: A 9-week theme might be long and laborious, and it can create a new problem of difficulty in integrating the variety of literature genres. In the example from Table 3.3, the three heaviest genres of realistic fiction, biography (autobiography), and

Table 3.5
Possible Concept Themes Organized by Major Social Studies Topics

Concept Themes	Geography	Native Americans	Economics	Colonization and Settlement	American Revolution	United States Constitution
	Adaptation	Adaptation	Adaptation	Adaptation	Augmentation	Beliefs
	Change	Augmentation	Communication	Augmentation	Beliefs	Change
	Environment	Beliefs	Cooperation	Beliefs	Change	Communication
	Exploration	Change	Ethics	Change	Conflict	Cooperation
	Immigration	Community	Exploration	Community	Context	Creation
	Interaction	Conflict	Interaction	Continuity	Continuity	Ethics
	Interconnection	Continuity	Leadership	Cooperation	Courage	Expression
	Migration	Cooperation	Order	Courage	Expression	Identity
	Movement	Culture	Power	Culture	Honor	Interaction
	Patterns	Diversity	Structure	Environment	Identity	Interdependence
	Perspective	Environment		Exploration	Interaction	Justice
	Population	Ethics		Immigration	Justice	Leadership
	Symbolism	Extinction		Interaction	Leadership	Order
	Survival	Identity		Interdependence	Order	Principles
		Interaction		Movement	Perspective	Relationships
		Interdependence		Order	Power	Rights
		Migration		Perspective	Revolution	Systems
		Order		Population	Rights	Values
		Perception		Relationships	Values	

68

Table 3.5, continued

Concept Themes, *continued*	Geography	Native Americans	Economics	Colonization and Settlement	American Revolution	United States Constitution
		Perspective Relationships Social Roles Survival Symbolism Traditions Values		Structure Systems Survival Social Roles Traditions Values		

Table 3.6
Cross-Curricular Connections of Social Studies Topics and C3 Framework for Social Studies

Theme	Social Studies	Science
Change *Interaction* *Movement*	Geography • Geographic Representations • Global Interconnections • Human-Environment Interaction • Human Population	Matter and Energy in Organisms and Ecosystems • Cycles of Matter and Energy Transfer in Ecosystems • Energy in Chemical Processes and Everyday Life • Interdependent Relationships in Ecosystems • Organization for Matter and Energy Flow in Organisms
Change Continuity Interaction Order *Relationships*	Native Americans • Change, Continuity, and Context • Causation and Augmentation • Historical Sources and Evidence	Matter and Energy in Organisms and Ecosystems • Cycles of Matter and Energy Transfer in Ecosystems • Energy in Chemical Processes and Everyday Life • Interdependent Relationships in Ecosystems • Organization for Matter and Energy Flow in Organisms Structure and Properties of Matter • Structure and Properties of Matter Chemical Reactions
Interaction Order *Structure*	Economics • Economic Decision Making • Exchange and Markets • The Global Economy • The National Economy	Structure and Properties of Matter • Structure and Properties of Matter Chemical Reactions

Table 3.6, continued

Theme	Social Studies	Science
Adaptation Augmentation Change Continuity Environment Interaction Relationships Movement	Colonization and Settlement ♦ Causation and Augmentation ♦ Change, Continuity, and Context ♦ Historical Sources and Evidence ♦ Perspectives	Earth's Systems ♦ Earth Materials and Systems ♦ Human Impacts on Earth Systems ♦ The Roles of Water in Earth's Surface Processes
Augmentation *Change* Continuity Interaction	American Revolution ♦ Causation and Augmentation ♦ Change, Continuity, and Context ♦ Historical Sources and Evidence ♦ Perspectives	Earth's Systems ♦ Earth Materials and Systems ♦ Human Impacts on Earth Systems ♦ The Roles of Water in Earth's Surface Processes Space Systems: Stars and the Solar System ♦ Earth and the Solar System ♦ Types of Interactions ♦ The Universe and Its Stars
Change Creation Interaction Interdependence Order Relationships *Systems*	U. S. Constitution ♦ Civic and Political Institutions ♦ Participation and Deliberation: Applying Civic Virtues and Democratic Principles ♦ Processes, Rules, and Laws	Space Systems: Stars and the Solar System ♦ Earth and the Solar System ♦ Types of Interactions ♦ The Universe and its Stars

adventure could be three of the units, with the fourth being a combination of prose, poetry, mythology, folklore, and stage plays. Now that the brainstorming of possible concept-based themes is complete, the next step is to decide the order of these concept-based themes. The subject of social studies often is taught in some sort of chronological order, although it can be taught by concept alone. The cause-and-effect nature of the subject matter can be very important, especially to those students (and teachers) who need to see information in a linear sequence. Table 3.7 identifies the themes from the science topics with the corresponding social studies topics. This table also treats each of the four major science units in a quarterly format.

Table 3.7 demonstrates how many common concepts are possible. Once a list of concepts is complete, the teacher planning the unit can look for parallels between the two subject areas. The core ideas of both subjects are included in an abbreviated format to make it easier to drill down to the main content. As mentioned several times, the social studies concepts often include potential themes. The themes of Augmentation and Continuity emerge as good possible choices based on the number of times each is identified in the grid. However, selecting a theme is not necessarily based on how frequently it shows up in a list of ideas. The teacher should think flexibly about how wide a big idea can expand, how it might tie best to students, and its transferability. In this example, other themes were determined to be used for these reasons. The choice of themes is up to the teacher, but in this case, the other themes allow for a greater span of options, including those that might address each of these unchosen concepts. Considering the content of the grade-level science and social studies topic, the chosen themes are italicized. These themes are the teacher's preliminary options. The teacher can examine how many opportunities are available to incorporate the content and standards with these themes. In some instances, it might be difficult to discern a clear theme without going into more depth of understanding of the topic. In the first concept-based unit, Movement and Interaction are still under consideration—the teacher has not made a decision as to which to use. This should become clearer as the unit developer works through the upcoming steps in the planning process. When other subject area content in language arts and potentially mathematics is included, the best concept will likely emerge.

Table 3.8 creates a succinct picture of six units. Notice that two of the science topics cross over into two units. As stated earlier, having these topics falling into two units helps students to interact with the content through multiple conceptual views.

Table 3.7
Common Concept–Based Themes in Social Studies and Science (Grade 5)

	Matter and Energy in Organisms and Ecosystems	Structure and Properties of Matter	Earth's Systems	Space Systems: Stars and the Solar System
Geography	Change Interaction Movement	Change Interaction Movement	Adaptation Change Environment Movement	Change Exploration Interaction
Native Americans	Change Continuity Interaction Order Relationships	Change Continuity Interaction Order Relationships	Adaptation Augmentation Change Continuity Diversity Environment Interaction Relationships	Augmentation Change Continuity Diversity Environment Interaction Interdependence Order Relationships
Economics	Interaction Order Structure	Interaction Order Structure	Adaptation Interaction	Interaction Order

Table 3.7, continued

	Matter and Energy in Organisms and Ecosystems	Structure and Properties of Matter	Earth's Systems	Space Systems: Stars and the Solar System
Colonization and Settlement	Continuity Change Interaction Interdependence Movement Order Relationships	Change Continuity Interdependence Interaction Movement Order Relationships	Adaptation Augmentation Change Continuity Environment Interaction Movement Relationships	Augmentation Change Continuity Environment Exploration Interaction Interdependence Order Relationships Structure Systems
American Revolution	Change Continuity Interaction Order	Change Continuity Interaction Order	Augmentation Change Continuity Interaction	Augmentation Change Continuity Interaction Order

Table 3.7, continued

	Matter and Energy in Organisms and Ecosystems	Structure and Properties of Matter	Earth's Systems	Space Systems: Stars and the Solar System
U.S. Constitution	Change Interaction Order Relationships	Change Interaction Order Relationships	Creation Interaction	Change Creation Interdependence Interaction Order Relationships Systems

Table 3.8
Six Final Units in Basic Form (Grade 5)

Theme	Social Studies	Science
Movement/ Interaction	Geography • Geographic Representations • Global Interconnections • Human-Environment Interaction • Human Population	Matter and Energy in Organisms and Ecosystems • Cycles of Matter and Energy Transfer in Ecosystems • Energy in Chemical Processes and Everyday Life • Interdependent Relationships in Ecosystems • Organization for Matter and Energy Flow in Organisms
Relationships	Native Americans • Causation and Augmentation Change, Continuity, and Context • Historical Sources and Evidence	Matter and Energy in Organisms and Ecosystems (first 3 weeks) • Cycles of Matter and Energy Transfer in Ecosystems • Energy Flow in Organisms • Energy in Chemical Processes and Everyday Life • Organization for Matter and • Interdependent Relationships in Ecosystems Structure and Properties of Matter (second 3 weeks) • Structure and Properties of Matter Chemical Reactions

Table 3.8, continued

Theme	Social Studies	Science
Structure	Economics ◆ Economic Decision Making ◆ Exchange and Markets ◆ The Global Economy ◆ The National Economy	Structure and Properties of Matter ◆ Structure and Properties of Matter Chemical Reactions
Adaptation	Colonization and Settlement ◆ Causation and Augmentation Change, Continuity, and Context ◆ Historical Sources and Evidence ◆ Perspectives	Earth's Systems ◆ Earth Materials and Systems ◆ Human Impacts on Earth Systems ◆ The Roles of Water in Earth's Surface Processes
Change	American Revolution ◆ Causation and Augmentation Change, Continuity, and Context ◆ Historical Sources and Evidence ◆ Perspectives	Earth's Systems (first 3 weeks) ◆ Earth Materials and Systems ◆ Human Impacts on Earth Systems ◆ The Roles of Water in Earth's Surface Processes Space Systems: Stars and the Solar System (second 3 weeks) ◆ Earth and the Solar System ◆ Types of Interactions ◆ The Universe and Its Stars

Table 3.8, continued

Theme	Social Studies	Science
Systems	U. S. Constitution • Applying Civic Virtues and Democratic Principles • Civic and Political Institutions • Participation and Deliberation • Processes, Rules, and Laws	Space Systems: Stars and the Solar System • Earth and the Solar System • Types of Interactions • The Universe and Its Stars

The final step is to add the language arts content and skills, as demonstrated in Table 3.9. Now that the decisions have been made to blend the corresponding social studies and science content together, the mapped-out English language arts can be added.

In reviewing the addition of the language arts topics and content, the teacher has made some adjustments, which are italicized in Table 3.9. The first was to include writing an opinion with the speaking skill of presenting an opinion. Not only does this have a content-related connection of expressing opinions, but it also comes during the second semester. Students will revisit the topic and present an opinion as a natural application of the skill, which validates the higher order thinking of a concept-based unit. The second adjustment was to flip the content between the themes of Structure and Adaptation. Many of the suggested adventure story novels have an evident theme of Adaptation. This change also allows for all three writing foci to be taught and applied each half of the school year. The final adjustment is the decision to use Interaction instead of Movement as the first theme. Once realistic fiction was added as the reading genre, it made this theme more appropriate, especially when considering the suggested literature selections.

The next chapter progresses to the resulting steps of creating enduring understandings and developing essential questions using Wiggins and McTighe's (2005) *Understanding by Design*.

Table 3.9

Final Six Units With English Language Arts Added and Then Adjusted

Theme	Social Studies	Science	Language Arts
Interaction	Geography ◆ Geographic Representations ◆ Global Interconnections ◆ Human–Environment Interaction ◆ Human Population	Matter and Energy in Organisms and Ecosystems ◆ Cycles of Matter and Energy Transfer in Ecosystems ◆ Energy in Chemical Processes and Everyday Life ◆ Interdependent Relationships in Ecosystems ◆ Organization for Matter and Energy Flow in Organisms	Realistic Fiction Write Narratives Summarize Written Text Information Presentations in Diverse Media and Formats
Relationships	Native Americans ◆ Causation and Augmentation ◆ Change, Continuity, and Context ◆ Historical Sources and Evidence	Matter and Energy in Organisms and Ecosystems (first 3 weeks) ◆ Cycles of Matter and Energy Transfer in Ecosystems ◆ Energy in Chemical Processes and Everyday Life ◆ Interdependent Relationships in Ecosystems ◆ Organization for Matter and Energy Flow in Organisms	Biographies and Autobiographies Write Opinion Pieces Engage in Collaborative Discussions

Table 3.9, continued

Theme	Social Studies	Science	Language Arts
Relationships, *continued*		Structure and Properties of Matter • Structure and Properties of Matter Chemical Reactions	*Narrative and Free Verse Poetry and Limerick* *Write Informative or Explanatory Texts* *Summarize Speakers' Points with Reasons and Evidence*
Structure	Economics • Economic Decision Making • Exchange and Markets • The Global Economy The National Economy		
Adaptation	Colonization and Settlement • Causation and Augmentation • Change, Continuity, and Context • Historical Sources and Evidence • Perspectives	Earth's Systems • Earth Materials and Systems • Human Impacts on Earth Systems • The Roles of Water in Earth's Surface Processes	*Adventure Stories* *Write Narratives* *Multimedia and Visual Presentations*

Table 3.9, continued

Theme	Social Studies	Science	Language Arts
Change	American Revolution ◆ Causation and Augmentation ◆ Change, Continuity, and Context ◆ Historical Sources and Evidence ◆ Perspectives	Earth's Systems (first three weeks) ◆ Earth Materials and Systems ◆ Human Impacts on Earth Systems ◆ The Roles of Water in Earth's Surface Processes Space Systems: Stars and the Solar System (second three weeks) ◆ Earth and the Solar System ◆ Types of Interactions ◆ The Universe and its Stars	Folktales, Legends, Fables, Fantasies, and Myths Write Opinion Pieces *Report on Topic or Text/Present Opinion*
Systems	U. S. Constitution ◆ Civic and Political Institutions ◆ Participation and Deliberation: Applying Civic Virtues and Democratic Principles ◆ Processes, Rules, and Laws	Space Systems: Stars and the Solar System ◆ Earth and the Solar System ◆ Types of Interactions ◆ The Universe and Its Stars	Staged Plays Write Informative or Explanatory Texts Adapt Speech to Variety of Contexts and Tasks

Concept-Based Units and Rigor as an Instructional Shift

Marzano, in collaboration with the Learning Sciences Marzano Center, identified 13 essential skills to meet the rigorous Common Core State Standards (Marzano & Toth, 2014). The 13 essential strategies are listed in Table 3.10. These strategies have appeared in the highly regarded *Strategies That Work* publications.

Marzano and Toth (2014) communicated the importance of the level of rigor embedded in the CCSS:

> Teachers need to plan for not only what students should understand and be able to do by the end of the learning cycle, they need to scaffold their instruction from facts and details to robust generalizations and processes in order to reach these rigorous standards. As part of this clear progression of learning, students need more opportunities to apply their knowledge and make inferences based on what they are learning. The shift to rigorous standards also requires students to make and defend claims with sound evidence including grounds, backing, and qualifiers as part of utilizing the knowledge they acquire in class. (p. 16)

Gradual release is an excellent way to move learning from teacher dependency to student autonomy. Feedback should come not only from the instructor, but also from peers and self. Self-evaluation may begin at a young age and become more frequent as students progress through subsequent school years. At the conclusion of a learning cycle, students should be able to demonstrate the standard independently.

In an article for *Phi Delta Kappan* in 2009, Marzano cautioned teachers, administrators, and schools about limiting the use of these strategies. He made these points:

1. *Do not focus on a narrow range of strategies*: Although the strategies are effective, they should not be the only ones to be implemented. Teaching is a very complex process and should be limited to a small number of approaches.
2. *Do not assume that high-yield strategies must be used in every class*: Although a teacher should have a collection of effective, go-to instructional approaches, one cannot expect to see a single strategy used by every teacher with the same success. Some subjects and classrooms lend themselves better to some strategies compared to others.

Table 3.10

Thirteen Essential Instructional Strategies to Achieve Rigor (Marzano & Toth, 2014)

1. Identifying critical content	The critical information or skills are identified in a unit and then reviewed and highlighted throughout. This allows the teacher and students to focus and serves as a foundation for building future skills with greater complexity.
2. Previewing new content	Students access prior knowledge to understand new content. This promotes comparison between what content is already known and what is new.
3. Organizing students to interact with content	Students are grouped to facilitate interaction and content. Implementation of appropriate cooperative learning structures is essential. Teachers organize the lesson and students in ways that promote cognitive and connotative skills.
4. Helping students process content	Student groups are systematically engaged in a student-centered classroom. As the facilitator, the teacher supports students as they work with summarizing and elaborating content.
5. Helping students elaborate on content	Students focus on providing evidence to support the inferences they are expected to make through summarizing and elaboration. This strategy is adaptable to any subject.
6. Helping students record and represent knowledge	True evidence of student learning is their own representation of their understanding of the content. Examples of this evidence are mental models, mathematical models, or other abstract interpretations of the content.
7. Managing response rates with tiered questioning techniques	Questions are proposed from baseline levels to higher thinking order to support students. Students are expected to provide evidence for their thinking.
8. Reviewing content	This strategy highlights previously learned content and skills that are cumulative in nature. The focus is on students being aware of the "big picture" of the critical content.

Table 3.10, continued

9. Helping students practice skills, strategies, and processes	Rigorous standards require students to be fluent and have different ways of demonstrating proficiency and implementing procedures. Students demonstrate increased confidence and competence.
10. Helping students examine similarities and differences	Students classify, categorize, compare, and analyze in order to speak to the "big ideas" and conclusions regarding the specific details. This should occur before, during, and after the learning experiences with an emphasis on deeper thinking.
11. Helping students examine their reasoning	Students are producing and defending claims from logical reasoning as a result of rigorous standards. Analyzing errors and misconceptions, as well as critiquing the logic of self and others, is necessary and aligns with the precision of the standards.
12. Helping students revise knowledge	Students critically compare prior knowledge with newly acquired knowledge. Students also look at knowledge from multiple perspectives as active and engaged learners.
13. Helping students engage in cognitive tasks	Teachers ensure that there are frequent complex tasks throughout a unit of study. These become more rigorous from the first opportunity through the last.

3. *Do not assume that high-yield strategies will always work*: It is important to know when an instructional strategy is being implemented by a compliant teacher and when it is helping to reach a desired result. There is a point when the teacher knows that it is time to adapt or even abandon an approach.

There are certainly correlations to the rigor of a concept-based unit, Common Core State Standards, and Marzano's (2009) high-yield strategies, but as Marzano pointed out, these high-yield strategies should not be seen as the only ones. Instead they should be used appropriately in context of the lessons and units. Curriculum mapping and concept-based units are the science of teaching-because they are developed based on the standards of what students should know, do, and understand. The strategies are the artistic side of instruction. A teacher designs the lessons based on good instructional practices and considers the non-scientific elements of the classroom dynamics, such as classroom composition, readiness for learning, and other essentials that make the learning environment unique. Bringing together the science and artistry of teaching creates a solid concept-based unit grounded in best instructional practices.

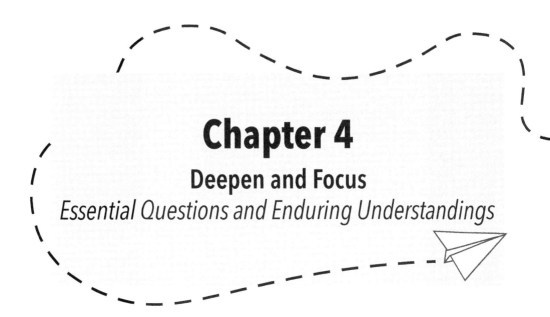

Chapter 4
Deepen and Focus
Essential Questions and Enduring Understandings

As presented in Chapter 1, Drake and Burns (2004) provided questions for designers to follow when developing a concept unit (see pp. 10–11). All of these are relevant and need to be considered, but the question regarding an interdisciplinary framework is the most important in developing a concept-based unit: *Can standards be organized in meaningful ways that cut across the curriculum?* Many of today's textbooks include at least one essential question in the lesson plan. Integrating these in widely published textbooks became popular after more and more educators learned of the work of Wiggins and McTighe (2005) through national presentations and publications. These essential questions serve as an overarching focus in the short term. In a concept-based unit lasting approximately 6 weeks, educators developing these questions should consider the cross-curricular and broad-based scope. Making questions too narrow reduces the flexibility of the wide-ranging thinking desired in the classroom.

With all-encompassing themes across an integrated unit of study, the development of the overarching essential questions and enduring understandings comes more naturally. Teachers who tend to have part-to-whole thinking may find it challenging. A suggested idea is to review the identified themes, the subject-area content, and the literature choices as a means for creating these units. The theme of Interaction (see Table 4.1) includes the topics of Geography in Social Studies, and Matter and Energy in Organisms and Ecosystems in

DOI:10.4324/9781003233770-6

Table 4.1

Interaction Theme With Relevant Subject Areas and Topics

Theme	Social Studies	Science	Language Arts
Interaction	Geography • Geographic Representations • Global Interconnections • Human-Environment Interaction • Human Population	Matter and Energy in Organisms and Ecosystems • Cycles of Matter and Energy Transfer in Ecosystems • Energy in Chemical Processes and Everyday Life • Interdependent Relationships in Ecosystems • Organization for Matter and Energy Flow in Organisms	Realistic Fiction • *Superfudge* (Judy Blume) • *The Best School Year Ever* (Barbara Robinson) • *Safe at Home* (Mike Lupica) Write Narratives Summarize Written Text Information Presentations in Diverse Media and Formats

Science. Language Arts would include students interacting with Realistic Fiction, Writing Narratives, and Summarizing Written Text Information Presentations in Diverse Media and Formats.

In addition, the following essential questions and enduring understandings from Table 4.1 would be produced.

Essential Questions:

1. How do various interactions change the course of a relationship for better or worse?
2. What creates an interaction?
3. When an interaction takes place, what are the subsequent events that may happen as a result?

Enduring Understandings:

1. Without interaction, there is absence of connection between and among forces and elements.
2. Interactions can create a cause-and-effect relationship that can be beneficial or detrimental.

3. The interactions one has with others may lead to taking future actions in various settings, relationships, events, and scientific phenomena.

In addition to these predominant essential questions and enduring understandings, topical questions and understandings are needed. These are more specific to the standards within each content area within the unit. Wiggins and McTighe (2005) organized this process into three stages:

1. Identify the desired results (e.g., the goals, content standards, and curriculum expectations).

2. Determine acceptable evidence. How will the student demonstrate understanding (e.g., test, performance task, written assignment, and formative tasks provided during the learning)?

3. Plan the learning experiences and instruction (e.g., facts, concepts, principles, products, procedures, strategies, sequence of the lessons, and teaching methods).

Tables 4.2–4.6 give examples of potential ways to assess the learning. Note that these can be used with intended core assessments, such as the basal reader, or with performance tasks judged against set criteria. These are just examples and not comprehensive. The school, the district, and grade-level appropriateness will greatly influence the assessment instrument used.

Concept-Based Teaching Through Visible Learning

Through a synthesis of research studies, Hattie found various influences in different meta-analyses according to Cohen's *d* scale of effect size. In Hattie's (2012) ground-breaking *Visible Learning for Teachers*, he ranked 138 influences impacting learner outcomes—from very positive effects to very negative effects. Hattie found that the average effect size of all of the interventions he studied was .40. This standard became the center for determining what influences were adverse or encouraging. In reviewing the top rankings, there are several effects related to this process that align with concept-based teaching. These would include the most impactful influences, which are at an effect size greater than .7:

◈ **Teacher estimate of achievement:** This is what the teacher believes the student can accomplish or achieve.

◈ **Conceptual change programs:** These programs strengthen understanding by encouraging students to question their own (or society's) preconceived notions. They involve two main steps: (1) introducing students to

Concept-Based Instruction

Table 4.2

Unit Sample Demonstrating Understandings, Standards,
and Evidence of Learning (Literacy)

Topical Understandings	Common Core State Standards	Evidence of Learning
A successful reader is proficient with phonics and word analysis, and is fluent. A successful reader uses multiple strategies, including context clues, figurative language, and multiple meaning words.	RF.5.3 Know and apply grade-level phonics and word analysis skills in decoding words. RF.5.4 Read with sufficient accuracy and fluency to support comprehension. RL.5.4 Determine the meaning of words and phrases as they are used in a text, including figurative language such as metaphors and similes. L.5.4 Determine or clarify the meaning of unknown and multi-ple-meaning words and phrases based on grade 5 reading and content, choosing flexibly from a range of strategies. L.5.5 Demonstrate understand-ing of figurative language, word relationships, and nuances in word meanings. L.5.6 Acquire and use accurately grade-appropriate general aca-demic and domain-specific words and phrases, including those that signal contrast, addition, and other logical relationships (e.g., *however, although, nevertheless, similarly, moreover, in addition*).	Weekly reading assess-ments that include questions aligned to word analysis skills explicitly instructed and practiced independently. Weekly reading assess-ments that include questions aligned to reading strategies explicitly instructed and practiced independently.

Table 4.2, continued

Topical Understandings	Common Core State Standards	Evidence of Learning
A proficient reader uses text evidence to support literary devices within literary text. A proficient reader analyzes various points of view, makes comparisons, and understands how visual representations contribute to comprehension from larger pieces of narrative texts.	RL.5.1 Quote accurately from a text when explaining what the text says explicitly and when drawing inferences from the text. RL.5.2 Determine a theme of a story, drama, or poem from details in the text, including how characters in a story or drama respond to challenges or how the speaker in a poem reflects upon a topic; summarize the text. RL.5.3 Compare and contrast two or more characters, settings, or events in a story or drama, drawing on specific details in the text (e.g., how characters interact). RL.5.5 Explain how a series of chapters, scenes, or stanzas fits together to provide the overall structure of a particular story, drama, or poem. RL.5.6 Describe how a narrator's or speaker's point of view influences how events are described. RL.5.7 Analyze how visual and multimedia elements contribute to the meaning, tone, or beauty of a text (e.g., graphic novel, multimedia presentation of fiction, folktale, myth, poem).	Weekly reading assessments that include questions requiring students to cite text evidence as instructed and practiced independently. Weekly reading assessments that include questions aligned to literary devices explicitly instructed and practiced independently.

Concept-Based Instruction

Table 4.2, continued

Topical Understandings	Common Core State Standards	Evidence of Learning
	RI.5.2 Determine two or more main ideas of a text and explain how they are supported by key details; summarize the text.	
	RI.5.5 Compare and contrast the overall structure (e.g., chronology, comparison, cause/effect, problem/solution) of events, ideas, concepts, or information in two or more texts.	
	RI.5.6 Analyze multiple accounts of the same event or topic, noting important similarities and differences in the point of view they represent.	

Table 4.3

Unit Sample Demonstrating Understandings, Standards, and Evidence of Learning (Language)

Topical Understandings	Common Core State Standards	Evidence of Learning
A successful writer is proficient with parts of speech at an application level.	L.5.1 Demonstrate command of the conventions of standard English grammar and usage when writing or speaking. • L.5.1.A Explain the function of conjunctions, prepositions, and interjections in general and their function in sentences. • L.5.1.B Form and use the perfect (e.g., *I had walked; I have walked; I will have walked*) verb tenses. • L.5.1.C Use verb tense to convey various times, sequences, states, and conditions. • L.5.1.D Recognize and correct inappropriate shifts in verb tense. • L.5.1.E Use correlative conjunctions (e.g., *either/or, neither/ nor*).	Daily editing assignments focusing on each of these standards. Weekly editing assessments that include each of these standards.

Table 4.3, continued

Topical Understandings	Common Core State Standards	Evidence of Learning
A successful writer is proficient with writing mechanics at an application level. Writing assignments are evaluated against a rubric that includes a general or specific application.	L.5.2 Demonstrate command of the conventions of standard English capitalization, punctuation, and spelling when writing. • L.5.2.A Use punctuation to separate items in a series. • L.5.2.B Use a comma to separate an introductory element from the rest of the sentence. • L.5.2.C Use a comma to set off the words yes and no (e.g., *Yes, thank you*), to set off a tag question from the rest of the sentence (e.g., *It's true, isn't it?*), and to indicate direct address (e.g., *Is that you, Steve?*). • L.5.2.D Use underlining, quotation marks, or italics to indicate titles of works. • L.5.2.E Spell grade-appropriate words correctly, consulting references as needed. L.5.3 Use knowledge of language and its conventions when writing, speaking, reading, or listening. • L.5.3.A Expand, combine, and reduce sentences for meaning, reader/listener interest, and style.	Daily editing assignments focusing on each of these standards. Weekly editing assessments that include each of these standards. Writing assignments are evaluated against a rubric that includes a general or specific application.

Table 4.4

*Unit Sample Demonstrating Understandings, Standards,
and Evidence of Learning (Writing and Speaking)*

Topical Understandings	Common Core State Standards	Evidence of Learning
A successful reader is proficient with phonics, word analysis, and fluency. A successful reader uses multiple strategies, including context clues, figurative language, and multiple meaning words.	*Writing* W.5.3 Write narratives to develop real or imagined experiences or events using effective technique, descriptive details, and clear event sequences. • W.5.3.A Orient the reader by establishing a situation and introducing a narrator and/or characters; organize an event sequence that unfolds naturally. • W.5.3.B Use narrative techniques, such as dialogue, description, and pacing, to develop experiences and events or show the responses of characters to situations. • W.5.3.C Use a variety of transitional words, phrases, and clauses to manage the sequence of events. • W.5.3.D Use concrete words and phrases and sensory details to convey experiences and events precisely. • W.5.3.E Provide a conclusion that follows from the narrated experiences or events.	Weekly reading assessments that include questions aligned to word analysis skills explicitly instructed and practiced independently. Weekly reading assessments that include questions aligned to reading strategies explicitly instructed and practiced independently.

Table 4.4, continued

Topical Understandings	Common Core State Standards	Evidence of Learning
A proficient reader uses text evidence to support literary devices within literary texts. A proficient reader analyzes various points of view, makes comparisons, and analyzes how visual representations contribute to comprehension from larger pieces of narrative texts.	*Speaking* SL.5.2 Summarize a written text read aloud or information presented in diverse media and formats, including visually, quantitatively, and orally.	Weekly reading assessments that include questions requiring students to cite text evidence as instructed and practiced independently. Weekly reading assessments that include questions aligned to literary devices explicitly instructed and practiced independently.

Table 4.5

Unit Sample Demonstrating Understandings, Standards, and Evidence of Learning (Social Studies)

Topical Understandings	C3 Framework for Social Studies State Standards	Evidence of Learning
Maps are representations of larger areas or items and can be in a variety of forms.	*Geographic Representations: Spatial Views of the World* D2.Geo.1.3–5. Construct maps and other graphic representations of both familiar and unfamiliar places.	Construct a map to scale of an area (classroom, bedroom, playground, etc.).
The map scale can help readers interpret the details of locations and environments.	D2.Geo.2.3–5. Use maps, satellite images, photographs, and other representations to explain relationships between the locations of places and regions and their environmental characteristics. D2.Geo.3.3–5. Use maps of different scales to describe the locations of cultural and environmental characteristics.	Respond to questions from a variety of maps (satellite, population, topographical, etc.), including the interpretation of scale.
A proficient map reader can analyze cultural and environmental changes to explain new interactions of a cultural population.	*Human–Environment Interaction: Place, Regions, and Culture* D2.Geo.4.3–5. Explain how culture influences the way people modify and adapt to their environments. D2.Geo.5.3–5. Explain how the cultural and environmental characteristics of places change over time. D2.Geo.6.3–5. Describe how environmental and cultural characteristics influence population distribution in specific places or regions.	Respond to a series of questions interpreting and comparing population or cultural maps at a predetermined level of proficiency.

97

Table 4.5, continued

Topical Understandings	C3 Framework for Social Studies State Standards	Evidence of Learning
A proficient map reader can analyze cultural and environmental changes to explain new interactions of a cultural population.	*Human Population: Spatial Patterns and Movements* D2.Geo.7.3–5. Explain how cultural and environmental characteristics affect the distribution and movement of people, goods, and ideas. D2.Geo.8.3–5. Explain how human settlements and movements relate to the locations and use of various natural resources. D2.Geo.9.3–5. Analyze the effects of catastrophic environmental and technological events on human settlements and migration.	Respond to a series of questions interpreting and comparing population or cultural maps at a predetermined level of proficiency.
A proficient map reader can analyze cultural and environmental changes to explain new interactions of a cultural population.	*Global Interconnections: Changing Spatial Patterns* D2.Geo.10.3–5. Explain why environmental characteristics vary among different world regions. D2.Geo.11.3–5. Describe how the spatial patterns of economic activities in a place change over time because of interactions with nearby and distant places. D2.Geo.12.3–5. Explain how natural and human-made catastrophic events in one place affect people living in other places.	Respond to a series of questions interpreting and comparing population or cultural maps at a predetermined level of proficiency.

Table 4.6

Unit Sample Demonstrating Understandings, Standards, and Evidence of Learning (Science)

Topical Understandings*	Standards Connections NGSS		Evidence of Learning
Creating models communicates ideas and concepts of scientific phenomena.	◆ 5–PS3–1 ◆ 5–LS1–1 ◆ 5–LS2–1		Students reproduce the transfer of energy from the sun to food with an accurate written or oral description defending how air and water are necessary for plant growth.
An ecosystem is a complexity of dependent elements that create a cycle of life.	◆ 5–PS3–1 ◆ 5–LS1–1 ◆ 5–LS2–1		Students create a model of the life cycle.
Stored energy is converted into a desired form for practical use.	◆ 5–PS3–1 ◆ 5–LS2–1		Students complete a diagram of how plant leaves absorb energy from the sun.
The energy released by burning fuel or digesting food was once energy from the sun that was captured by plants in the chemical process that forms plant matter (from air and water).	◆ 5–PS3–1 ◆ 5–LS1–1 ◆ 5–LS2–1		Students explain how energy from food is absorbed and stored for later use in the body.

* Some topical understandings are drawn from the NGSS.

Table 4.6, continued

Topical Understandings*	Standards Connections NGSS—CCSS for ELA	Evidence of Learning
Animals and plants generally take in air and water. Animals must take in food, and plants need light and minerals. Anaerobic life, such as bacteria in the gut, functions without air. Food provides animals with materials for body repair and growth. Plants acquire their material for growth from air and water and process matter they have formed to maintain their internal conditions.	• RI.5.1 (5-LS1-1) • RI.5.7 (5-PS3-1, 5-LS2-1) • RI.5.9 (5-LS1-1) • W.5.1 (5-LS1-1) • SL.5.5 (5-PS3-1, 5-LS2-1)	Students explain how animals use food and provide examples and evidence that support each type of use, including diagrams and an argument with evidence. Evidence for growth and repair should include use of some of food's weight in the process of adding body weight or tissue. Evidence for energy use should refer to the need for energy transfer in performing the activity.

Table 4.6, continued

Topical Understandings*	Standards Connections NGSS—CCSS for Math	Evidence of Learning
The food of animals can be traced back to plants. Organisms are related in food webs in which some animals eat plants for food and other animals eat the animals that eat plants. Some organisms break down dead organisms. Decomposition restores materials back to the soil for plants to use. Organisms can survive in particular environments. A healthy ecosystem is one in which multiple species of different types are each able to meet their needs in a relatively stable web of life; newly introduced species can damage the balance of an ecosystem.	◆ MP2 (5-LS1-1, 5-LS2-1) ◆ MP4 (5-LS1-1, 5-LS2-1) ◆ MP5 (5-LS1-1) ◆ 5.MD.A.1 (5-LS1-1)	Create a food web using correct examples of each stage. Given a correct food web, explain what would happen if one element was missing and what would happen if another predator was added to the web. Complete a multiple-choice assessment over decomposition and organism survival.
Matter cycles between the air and soil and among plants, animals, and microbes as these organisms live and die. Organisms obtain gases, water, and minerals from the environment and release waste matter (gas, liquid, or solid) back into the environment.	◆ MP2 (5-LS1-1, 5-LS2-1) ◆ MP4 (5-LS1-1, 5-LS2-1) ◆ MP5 (5-LS1-1) ◆ 5.MD.A.1 (5-LS1-1)	Given a diagram of a plant, label the exchanges of oxygen, carbon dioxide, water, sunlight, and minerals.

101

new concepts and ideas, and (2) asking students to think about common misconceptions that might contradict these new concepts.

❖ **Transfer of learning:** This is learning in one context and then applying it to another, as well as the capacity to apply acquired knowledge and skills to new situations.

❖ **Concepting mapping:** This is demonstrating relationships between concepts and ideas. These are often graphic shapes with words used to connect the relationship.

The following mindframes from Hattie and Zierer's (2018) *10 Mindframes for Visible Learning: Teaching With Success* complement the most impactful effect, teacher estimate of achievement:

1. I'm an evaluator of my impact on student learning.
2. I see assessment as informing my impact and next steps.
3. I collaborate with all about my conceptions of progress and my impact.
4. I am a change agent and believe all students can improve.
5. I strive for challenge and not merely "doing your best."
6. I give feedback and act on feedback given to me.
7. I engage as much in dialogue as monologue.
8. I inform students what successful impact looks like.
9. I build relationships and trust.
10. I focus on learning and the language of learning. (p. 7)

Hattie has been cited in works authored by Wiggins and others. In Tomlinson, Moon, and Imbeau's (2015) white paper, *Assessment and Student Success in a Differentiated Classroom*, the works of Erickson, Hattie, and Wiggins and McTighe served as the springboard. Tomlinson et al. concluded that a high-quality curriculum is a synthesis of these works. These ideas come together to create rich and engaging units of study. By using the conglomeration of these principles and ideas, students will learn more, make greater connections, and be able to apply what they have learned in new and more complex situations. Teachers plan for learner engagement by designing lessons that bring out curiosity and tap into students' natural desire to learn. Lessons should also relate to students' lives and connect to previous experiences. In addition, students need to grapple with "just right" challenges to make sense of the content. Students should be shown the links between disciplines and make neurological, psychological, and social connections.

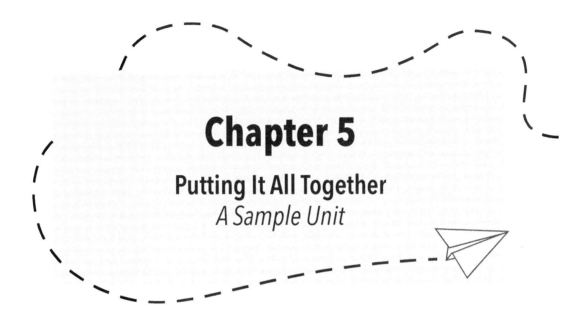

Chapter 5

Putting It All Together
A Sample Unit

This chapter takes the concepts shared in the previous chapters to provide an example of a concept-based unit. Keep in mind that this unit can evolve and change each year it is implemented to be more effective than the year before. The templates shared in this chapter demonstrate the overall picture of the unit, followed by more specific details in each subject. Table 5.1 is an example of one teacher's classroom themes. This teacher identifies Interdependence as the overarching theme for the year and ties it to a second layer of concept development with the other six units.

The learning for the language mechanics and conventions is assessed based on the use of two bell-ringer sentences each morning when students arrive. These sentences focus on the language and conventions standards and spiral throughout the year. There should be a weekly emphasis in a skill area. For example, the teacher could include a sentence that needs commas in a series. This sentence could include misplaced commas as well as too many commas. This exercise demonstrates how well a student knows how to demonstrate a skill. The assessment that week would require students to position commas accurately, and students would continue to practice that skill all year long. The teacher would evaluate students' proficiency against the school's writing evaluation tool.

Table 5.2 demonstrates a completed 6-week unit. The top of the table identifies the concept theme of Interactions followed by an optional unit name, Making

 DOI:10.4324/9781003233770-7

Concept-Based Instruction

Table 5.1

Yearlong Concept-Based Themes From a Real Classroom

Interdependence		
Adaptations	Challenges	Change
Diversity	Influence	Conflict

Connections. Some teachers like to use a different name for a unit rather than the name of the concept theme. The last item for the first row is the anticipated dates of implementation. The second row identifies the essential questions and enduring understandings, which will be the focus throughout the unit. Three columns are created identifying the contents of social studies, science, and English language arts. If mathematics or other classes, such as music, world language, visual art, or physical education, were added, then additional columns would be needed. Within each of these columns, teachers would outline what students are to know, understand, and be able to do, and would determine what evidence is expected to demonstrate that learning, just like the core subjects. To become more specific, Bloom's revised taxonomy (Anderson & Krathwohl, 2001), Webb's (1999) Depth of Knowledge level, and Marzano's (2009) effective strategies have been included. The following serves as a key to the codes used:

Bloom's taxonomy:
- ❖ Rem: Remembering
- ❖ Und: Understand
- ❖ App: Application
- ❖ Ana: Analyze
- ❖ Eval: Evaluate
- ❖ Cre: Create

Webb's Depth of Knowledge (DOK):
- ❖ 1: Recall and Reproduction
- ❖ 2: Skills and Concepts
- ❖ 3: Strategic Thinking
- ❖ 4: Extended Thinking

Marzano's Essentials for Achieving Rigor:
- ❖ 1: Identifying critical content
- ❖ 2: Previewing new content
- ❖ 3: Organizing students to interact with critical content
- ❖ 4: Helping students process content
- ❖ 5: Helping students elaborate content
- ❖ 6: Helping students record and represent content

❖ 7: Managing response rates with tiered questioning techniques
❖ 8: Reviewing content
❖ 9: Helping students practice skills, strategies, and processes
❖ 10: Helping students examine similarities and differences
❖ 11: Helping students examine their reasoning
❖ 12: Helping students revise knowledge
❖ 13: Helping students engage in cognitively complex tasks

The Evidence of Learning column in social studies indicates that the expected Bloom's order of thinking is at a Remembering level incorporated with Webb's DOK 1 of recalling and reproduction. The interpretation of Marzano's essential skills to achieving academic rigor would include organizing students with critical content and helping students practice skills, strategies, or processes. Evidence of Learning is coded in the same way throughout this table.

There are six indicators in the literacy and reading skills portion of Table 5.2: Reading Informational (RI) text, Reading Foundations (RF), Reading Literature (RL), Language (L), Writing (W), and Speaking and Listening (SL). An easy mistake a teacher may make in integrating authentic and high-quality text is neglecting to include the actual skills or standards (i.e., what students are expected to know and understand). The suggested format is to rotate four of these skills expectations each week, with students citing text evidence associated with the comprehension skill. The phonics and word analysis skills should also be practiced each week and can hopefully be tied to the literature students are reading. For the informational text standards, the teacher may incorporate not only social and science content, but also content referenced in the narrative literature from the authentic texts. An example would be students reading *Superfudge*, a children's novel by Judy Blume. Students would then read nonfiction texts about New York City, NY, and Princeton, NJ, which are both referenced in the book. Students could compare the two cities as identified in CCSS.ELA-Literacy. RI.5.5. Similarly, in the novel *Bud, Not Buddy*, students could research and compare cities in Michigan. Note how this example includes the social studies focus of maps and geography. Students might also read about the Great Depression and use it as a research topic or as a historical setting for narrative writing. In James Howe's *The Misfits*, the fictional setting is similar to the town where Howe grew up in upstate New York. This is an opportunity to compare the geographical areas of New York state, with its extreme differences between the cosmopolitan city and the northeastern climate and land features.

This example is also an opportunity to have two different levels of readers working together on something in common. *The Misfits* group could also take what they learned about northern New York along Lake Ontario and the Great Lakes bordering Michigan, and make a second comparison with the students

Table 5.2

Sample Unit With Overview of Aligned Common Core State Standards—What Will Students Know, Understand, and Be Able to Do With Evidence? (Grade 5)

Concept Theme: Interaction—Grade 5	Unit Name: Making Connections	Dates: 6 Weeks (September 4–October 13)
Essential Questions: 1. How do various interactions change the course of a relationship for better or worse? 2. What creates an interaction? 3. When an interaction takes place, what are the subsequent events that may happen as a result?		Enduring Understandings: 1. Without interaction, there is an absence of connection between and among forces and elements. 2. Interactions can create a cause-and-effect relationship that can be beneficial or detrimental. 3. The interactions one has with others may lead to taking future actions.

Social Studies Topic: Geography

Standards Emphasized:

C3 Framework: D2.Geo.1.3–5, D2.Geo.2.3–5, D2.Geo.3.3–5, D2.Geo.4.3–5, D2.Geo.5.3–5, D2.Geo.6.3–5, D2.Geo.7.3–5, D2.Geo.8.3–5, D2.Geo.9.3–5, D2.Geo.10.3–5, D2.Geo.11.3–5, D2.Geo.12.3–5

CCSS Mathematics

5.GA.1

Science Topic: Matter and Energy (through plants)

Standards Emphasized (first 6 weeks of 9):

NGSS 5-PS3-1, 5-LS1-1, 5-LS2-1

CCSS Mathematics

MP2, MP4, MP5

5.MD.A.1

CCSS Literacy

RI.5.1, RI.5.7, RI.5.9, W.5.1, SL.5.5

Language Arts Topic(s): Genre (Realistic Fiction): *Superfudge* (Judy Blume), *Bud, Not Buddy* (Christopher Paul Curtis), *The Misfits* (James Howe), Writing Narratives, and Information Presentations in Diverse Media and Formats

Standards Emphasized:

CCSS RF.5.1, RF.5.4, RL.5.1, RL.5.2, RL.5.3, RL.5.4, RL.5.5, RL.5.6, RL.5.7, RI.5.5, RI.5.6, L.5.1, L.5.2, L.5.3, L.5.4, L.5.5, L.5.6, W.5.3, SL.5.2

Table 5.2, continued

Social Studies Topic: Geography

Students Will Know	Evidence of Learning
Lines of latitude and longitude are measured in degrees of a circle.	Use a circular protractor to locate positions on a circle. *Bloom: Rem* *Webb DOK: 1* *Marzano: 3, 9*
Places can be precisely located where these lines intersect.	Locate locations in all four hemispheres using coordinates. *Bloom: Rem* *Webb DOK: 1* *Marzano: 3, 9*
Location can be stated in terms of degrees north or south of the equator and east or west of the prime meridian.	Use an adapted Cartesian coordinate plane to find locations on the x- and y-axes. *Bloom: Rem* *Webb DOK: 1* *Marzano: 3, 9*

Science Topic: Matter and Energy

Students Will Know	Evidence of Learning
Familiar living things need water, food, and air to help them survive.	After experiencing text and media information, students will identify the need for water, food, and air for survival at a predetermined level of mastery. *Bloom: App* *Webb DOK: 1* *Marzano: 1, 6, 11, 13*
How the sun is important for life on Earth.	Identify that the sun warms the Earth's surface through comparison of temperature of objects in the shade compared to direct sunlight. *Bloom: Under* *Webb DOK: 2* *Marzano: 1, 5, 10*

Language Arts Topic(s)

Students Will Know	Evidence of Learning
Accurately use the grade-level phonics and word analysis skills.	Respond to questions on weekly assessments with accuracy at a predetermined proficiency. *Bloom: Rem, Under* *Webb DOK: 1, 3*
Accurately use targeted context clues, figurative language, and/or multiple meaning words.	
Accurately use text evidence, analyze points of view, and make comparisons.	
Identify the seven parts of speech in declarative and interrogative sentences. Form verbs in the perfect verb tense; use verbs to convey various times, sequences, states, and conditions.	Given declarative or interrogative sentences, identify any given part of speech at a predetermined proficiency level. *Bloom: Rem, Under* *Webb DOK: 1, 2*

Table 5.2, continued

Students Will Understand	Evidence of Learning
Social Studies Topic: Geography	
Maps are larger representations of larger areas or items.	Construct a map to scale of an area. *Bloom: App* *Webb DOK: 3* *Marzano: 4, 10*
A map's scale can interpret the details of locations and environments.	Respond to questions from a variety of maps. *Bloom: Under* *Webb DOK: 2, 3*
Maps describe adaptation and how cultures adapted to variations in the physical environment.	Describe how the environment influences structure of shelter and dependence on regional food sources. *Bloom: Under* *Webb DOK: 1* *Marzano: 2, 3*
Maps describe specific physical features that influenced historical events and movements.	a.) Explain how waterways, bodies of water, and land features create boundaries. *Bloom: Under* *Webb DOK: 2* *Marzano: 4, 11*

Students Will Know	Evidence of Learning
Science Topic: Matter and Energy	
What is unique to different species of animals to help them survive.	Through various media forms provided by the teacher, students will accurately identify that animals have a living cycle of birth, growth and death and external parts to help them survive, grow and meet their needs. *Bloom: Under* *Webb DOK: 1* *Marzano: 4, 5*
Plants need sunlight and water to grow.	Through investigation with water and sunlight as variables, use plants to draw accurate conclusions about the need for water and light. *Bloom: Under* *Webb DOK: 3* *Marzano: 4, 5*

Students Will Know	Evidence of Learning
Language Arts Topic(s)	
a.) Recognize inappropriate shifts in verb tense. b.) Use correlative conjunctions. c.) Use the standard English to correctly use commas in a series.	Proficiency on daily editing assignments emphasizing verbs tenses and correlative conjunctions. *Bloom: Rem/Under* *Webb DOK: 1*
a.) Use the standard English to correctly use commas to separate introductory elements from the rest of the sentence. b.) Use the standard English to correctly use commas to set off the words *yes, no,* and *well;* a direct address at the beginning or end of a sentence or set off a tag question from the rest of the sentence.	a.–b.) Proficiency on daily editing assignments emphasizing correct use of commas in a sentence. *Bloom: Under* *Webb DOK: 1* c.) Proficiency on daily editing assignments emphasizing correct use of underlining, quotations, and italics for titles of works. *Bloom: Under* *Webb DOK: 1*

Table 5.2, continued

Social Studies Topic: Geography

Students Will Understand	Evidence of Learning
	b.) Cite historical examples of when locations determined settlements. *Bloom: Ana* *Webb DOK: 1* *Marzano: 4, 5, 6*

Students Will Be Able to Do	Evidence of Learning
Analyze cultural and environmental changes to explain new interactions.	Respond to a series of questions interpreting and comparing population or cultural maps. *Bloom: App* *Webb DOK: 2* *Marzano: 8, 10*
Analyze how cultural and environmental changes explain new interactions of a cultural population.	Given a physical map, write an explanation of how climate waterways and landforms determine a culture's way of life. *Bloom: Under* *Webb DOK: 2* *Marzano: 5, 11*

Science Topic: Matter and Energy

Students Will Understand	Evidence of Learning
Creating models to communicate ideas and concepts of scientific phenomena.	Create a model of the sun transferring energy to support plant growth and how eating the plants helps animals to develop and change. *Bloom: App* *Webb DOK: 2* *Marzano: 1, 3, 5*
An ecosystem is a complexity of dependent elements that create a life cycle.	Independently apply the concept of matter, plants, animals, and decomposers in a diagram correctly. *Bloom: App* *Webb DOK: 2* *Marzano: 3, 4, 5*
Stored energy is converted into a desired form for practical use.	Use a graphic design to demonstrate how energy plants receive from the sun and are released as burned fuel or digestion. *Bloom: Under* *Webb DOK: 2* *Marzano: 4, 12*

Language Arts Topic(s)

Students Will Know	Evidence of Learning
c.) Use the standard English to correctly use underlining, quotations, or italics to indicate titles of works. d.) Use the standard English to correctly use grade-level spelling word correctly, including the use of references for unknown words.	d.) Demonstrate proficiency of grade-level spelling assessments and transferred to written assignments. *Bloom: Rem* *Webb DOK: 1*
Expand, combine, and reduce sentences for meaning.	Demonstrate proficiency through mini-lessons on each of these skills and transferred to written assignments and scored with the school writing rubric. *Bloom: Under* *Webb DOK: 2*

Table 5.2, continued

Students Will Understand	Evidence of Learning
Science Topic: Matter and Energy	
Animals and plants generally take in air and water, but anaerobic life functions without air.	Make a comparison chart among a plant, animal, and bacteria demonstrating the need or lack of need for air and water. *Bloom: Ana* *Webb DOK: 3* *Marzano: 4*
Organisms can survive in particular environments.	Using published sources on the topics of animal, plant, and anaerobic life environments, explain the findings explicitly. *Bloom: Under* *Webb DOK: 1*

Students Will Understand	Evidence of Learning
Language Arts Topic(s)	
A successful writer is proficient with parts of speech at an application level.	This trait of writing is scored at a proficient or higher rate of application. *Bloom: App* *Webb DOK: 1*
A successful writer is proficient with writing mechanics at an application level.	This trait of writing is scored at a proficient or higher rate of application. *Bloom: App* *Webb DOK: 1*
Writing assignments are evaluated against a rubric that includes a general or specific application.	Able to identify and describe each rubric element for each writing or piece. *Bloom: Under* *Webb DOK: 1*
Narrative writing assignments tell a story.	Using all or part of the elements of the rubric, the student would be at a proficient level with: a.) Establishing a situation and characters. *Bloom: App* *Webb DOK: 2, 3*

Table 5.2 continued

Students Will Be Able to Do	Evidence of Learning
Science Topic: Matter and Energy	
Emphasize that plant life growth comes from air and water—not the soil.	Create a table of examples of plants that grow with and without soil, using multiple print or media sources. *Bloom: Under* *Webb DOK: 2* *Marzano: 10*
Describe the movement of matter among plants, animals, decomposers, and the environment.	Develop a model demonstrating these concepts in a diagram or three-dimensional design. *Bloom: Ana* *Webb DOK: 2* *Marzano: 6, 8*

Students Will Understand	Evidence of Learning
Language Arts Topic(s)	
	b.) Using narrative writing techniques. c.) Using a variety of transitional words, phrases, and clauses to manage the sequence of events. *Bloom: Under* *Webb DOK: 1* d.) Using concrete words and phrases and sensory details to convey experiences and events precisely. *Bloom: Under* *Webb DOK: 2* e.) Providing a conclusion that follows from the narrated experiences or events. *Bloom: Under* *Webb DOK: 2*

Table 5.2, continued

Students Will Be Able to Do	Evidence of Learning
Language Arts Topic(s)	
Use visual representations to comprehend from larger pieces of narrative texts.	Choose a graphic representation that appropriately suits the literary device for the narrative text emphasized. *Bloom: Under* *Webb DOK: 3* *Marzano: 9, 11*
Use text evidence to support literary devices within the text.	Respond to questions on weekly assessments with accuracy at a pre-determined proficiency. *Bloom: Under* *Webb DOK: 1*
Write narratives.	Score the narrative writing piece against the provided rubric at a proficient level. *Bloom: App* *Webb DOK: 2* *Marzano: 11*

who read *Bud, Not Buddy* about the cities of Flint and Grand Rapids, MI, which are the main settings. In the end, these opportunities allow for cross-curricular connections. With good lesson reflection, students can be prompted to think about the unit theme and respond to the essential questions and enduring understandings with teacher guidance about the different points of view (CCSS.ELA-LITERACY.RI.5.6) in a transferrable learning design. Like this social studies example, science concepts should be integrated when natural and appropriate. Teachers can expect times when subjects might cross over better than others, but they should always be cognizant of planned and unexpected opportunities.

Table 5.3 is an outline of a 6-week unit. This skeleton is incomplete and requires specific standards, objective, learning activities, and assessments. It serves as a basic weekly outline of what students are experiencing for the week in each of the subjects. The unit's essential questions and enduring understandings serve as a reminder of the connections that teachers should make for deeper thinking across subject matter during the course of the unit.

The next phase is to get started in a sensible and intelligent manner. Working with colleagues may take the weight off of one teacher. After mapping out the curriculum and identifying the themes, teachers will be ready to implement. The first unit could draw from a subject area a teacher is passionate about or one that a teacher finds uninspiring or weak but hopes to make better. In addition, instead of taking on a full year, it is suggested that teachers complete one unit each semester and then add on one or two each during the following years until all six are completed. The unit creations will continue to be reviewed, revised, and executed. By taking manageable bites, success is assured.

Summary and Implications

Concept-based instruction involves taking the best ideas of educational theorists and creating rich, in-depth, cohesive, and meaningful learning experiences for students. Its design requires rigor, higher level thinking, and connectivity across disciplines. The original work of Erickson (2002) served as the framework and reference for other leading and well-respected educational theorists. Throughout this book, teachers have been guided in how to create units that accomplish integrated, connected, and meaningful content for student learning. Focusing on what students should know, understand, and be able to do is critical to the purposes of these units.

Teachers should plan to work smarter through collaborating with others. This will allow the ideas to flow and reduce those moments of feeling stumped. Collaboration can also clarify teachers' goals and maintain their focus. Although this book was primarily written from an elementary education perspective, it is

Concept-Based Instruction

Table 5.3
Skeletal Plan of a 6-Week Unit

Concept Theme: Interaction—Grade 5		Dates: 6 weeks (September 4–October 13)
Essential Questions: 1. How do various interactions change the course of a relationship for better or worse? 2. What creates an interaction? 3. When an interaction takes place, what are the subsequent events that may happen as a result?		**Enduring Understandings:** 1. Without interaction, there is an absence of connection between and among forces and elements. 2. Interactions can create a cause-and-effect relationship that can be beneficial or detrimental. 3. The interactions one has with others may lead to taking future actions.
Week of	**Social Studies**	**Science**	**Literacy**	**Writing**
Sept. 4	Latitude and longitude	Role of sunlight, water, and food for growth	• Phonics and word analysis skills • Quote text accurately • Theme • Compare/contrast (RL) • Points of view (RL) • Book components • Word meanings	• Daily language skills • Basic parts of speech

114

Table 5.3, continued

Concept Theme: Interaction–Grade 5		Dates: 6 weeks (September 4–October 13)		
Week of	Social Studies	Science	Literacy	Writing
Sept. 11	Reading political maps	Ecosystems	◆ Phonics and word analysis skills ◆ Quote text accurately ◆ Simile/metaphor ◆ Visual media ◆ Compare/contrast (RI) ◆ Points of view (RI)	◆ Daily language skills ◆ Basic parts of speech
Sept. 18	Reading physical maps	Models of how energy is transferred from the sun	◆ Phonics and word analysis skills ◆ Quote text accurately ◆ Theme ◆ Compare/contrast (RL) ◆ Points of view (RL) ◆ Book components ◆ Word meanings	◆ Daily language skills ◆ Establish narrative framework and rubric ◆ Writer's workshop—narratives

Table 5.3, continued

	Concept Theme: Interaction—Grade 5		Dates: 6 weeks (September 4–October 13)	
Week of	**Social Studies**	**Science**	**Literacy**	**Writing**
Sept. 25	Reading physical maps	Comparison chart of different life forms	• Phonics and word analysis skills ♦ Quote text accurately ♦ Simile/metaphor ♦ Visual media ♦ Compare/contrast (RI) ♦ Points of view (RI)	• Daily language skills ♦ Mini-lessons regarding transitional words ♦ Writer's workshop—narratives
Oct. 2	Analysis of cultural maps	Table of species of plants that grow with and without soil	• Phonics and word analysis skills ♦ Quote text accurately ♦ Theme ♦ Compare/contrast (RL) ♦ Points of view (RL) ♦ Book components ♦ Word meanings	• Daily language skills ♦ Mini-lessons regarding sensory words ♦ Writer's workshop—narratives
Oct. 9	Analysis of cultural maps	Transfer of matter in the ecosystem of life	• Simile/metaphor ♦ Visual media ♦ Compare/contrast (RI) ♦ Points of view (RI)	• Daily language skills ♦ Final narrative scored against rubric (self, peer, and teacher)

certainly adaptable to the secondary grade-level years. Imagine the connections students would make as they move from classroom to classroom and teacher to teacher.

During the middle years, the type and number of courses a student might take expand and diversify; however, it is likely that all students in a grade level will still take an English, math, science, and social studies course. It is common to expect a variation of academic levels to accommodate different learners, such as those with high ability, English language learners, or students receiving special education services. Although a feeling of disconnect can occur when subjects are treated separately at the secondary level, it does not have to be this way. Near the end of the high school experience, students prepare to enroll in vocational, college preparatory, or dual credit courses. Concept-based unit design can be done well at the secondary level as long as students have a core of universal subject matter. For example, imagine how eighth-grade students could make interdisciplinary connections around a central theme regardless of the time of day or instructor because all students take the same English, general science, and social studies courses. With a tightly woven concept-based unit plan, the connections are possible. A shift in thinking will be required for secondary schools, especially if a school has traditionally operated with limited articulation and communication across subjects. No matter how the units are created, the most important thing is how much students will learn in a cohesive, deep, and transformative environment.

The remaining pages of this book are appendices of resources for teachers to develop their own units. They include ideas of conceptual themes and templates for organizing yearly plans, 6-week units, and weekly maps. These resources maintain a focus on what students are to know, understand, and do. They also maintain a focus on the overarching essential questions and enduring understandings and allow opportunities for differentiation. Unit designers will find blank versions of the templates used throughout this book. These templates are created in a reproducible format that will allow teachers to develop their plans. These templates also serve as a means for getting started and adding more details as necessary. For example, some will find it easier to map out the year and add review standards and curriculum first. Others will choose to include the essential questions and enduring understandings after mapping. Regardless, teachers will make some revisions before the first unit is executed and will continue to revise during implementation and in the following years.

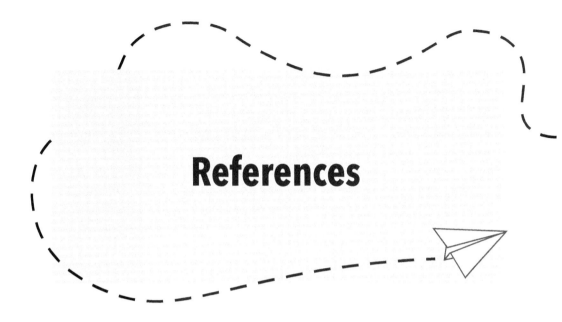

References

Anderson, L., & Krathwohl, D. R. (Eds.). (2001). *A taxonomy for learning, teaching, and assessing: A revision of Bloom's taxonomy of educational objectives* (Complete ed.). New York, NY: Longman.

Beecher, M., & Sweeny, S. (2008). Closing the achievement gap with curriculum enrichment and differentiation: One school's story. *Journal of Advanced Academics, 19*, 502–530.

Bloom, B. (Ed.). (1956). *Taxonomy of educational objectives: The classification of educational goals. Handbook I: Cognitive domain.* New York, NY: Longmans Green.

Bruner, J. (1996). *The culture of education.* Cambridge, MA: Harvard University Press.

Drake, S. M., & Burns, R. C. (2004). *Meeting standards through integrated curriculum.* Alexandria, VA: Association for Supervision and Curriculum Development.

DuFour, R. (2004). What is a professional learning community? *Educational Leadership, 61*(8), 6–11.

DuFour, R., DuFour, R., Eaker, R., & Many, T. (2006). *Learning by doing: A handbook for professional learning communities at work.* Bloomington, IN: Solution Tree.

Erickson, H. L. (2002). *Concept-based curriculum and instruction: Teaching beyond the facts.* Thousand Oaks, CA: Corwin.

Erickson, H. L. (2012). *Concept-based teaching and learning* [Position paper]. Washington, DC: International Baccalaureate Organization.

Erickson, H. L., Lanning, L. A., & French, R. (2017). *Concept-based curriculum and instruction for the thinking classroom* (2nd ed.). Thousand Oaks, CA: Corwin.

Hattie, J. (2012). *Visible learning for teachers: Maximizing impact on learning.* New York, NY: Routledge.

Hattie, J., & Zierer, K. (2018). *10 mindframes for visible learning: Teaching with success.* New York, NY: Routledge.

Hess, K., Jones, B., Carlock, D., & Walkup, J. (2009). *What exactly do "fewer, clearer, and higher standards" really look like in the classroom? Using a cognitive rigor matrix to analyze curriculum, plan lessons, and implement assessments.* Paper presented at the National Conference on Student Assessment, Council of Chief State School Officers, Detroit, MI.

Jacobs, H. H. (1997). *Mapping the big picture: Integrating curriculum and assessment K–12.* Alexandria, VA: Association for Supervision and Curriculum Development.

Kiernan, L. J. (Producer), & Bloom, G. (Director). (1997). *Differentiating instruction* [Video professional development series]. Alexandria, VA: Association for Supervision and Curriculum Development.

Lee, V., Smith, J., & Croninger, R. (1995). *Another look at high school restructuring. More evidence that it improves student achievement and more insight into why.* Madison: Center on Organization and Restructuring of Schools, School of Education, University of Wisconsin-Madison.

Marzano, R. J. (2009). Setting the record on 'high-yield' strategies. *Phi Delta Kappan, 91*(6), 30–37.

Marzano, R. J., Pickering, D. J., & Pollock, J. E. (2001). *Classroom instruction that works.* Alexandria, VA: Association for Supervision and Curriculum Development.

Marzano, R. J., & Toth, M. D. (2014). *Teaching for rigor: A call for a critical instructional shift.* West Palm Beach, FL: Learning Sciences International.

McLaughlin, M. W., & Talbert, J. E. (2001). *Professional communities and the work of high school teaching.* Chicago, IL: University of Chicago Press.

National Council for the Social Studies. (2010). *National curriculum standards for social studies: Executive summary.* Retrieved from https://www.socialstudies. org/standards/execsummary

National Council for the Social Studies. (2013). *The College, Career, and Civic Life (C3) Framework for Social Studies State Standards: Guidance for enhancing the rigor of K–12 civics, economics, geography, and history*. Silver Spring, MD: Author.

National Research Council. (2012). *A framework for K–12 science education: practices, crosscutting concepts, and core ideas*. Washington, DC: The National Academies Press. https://doi.org/10.17226/13165

Newmann, F., & Wehlage, G. (1995). *Successful school restructuring*. Madison: Center on Organization and Restructuring of Schools, School of Education, University of Wisconsin-Madison.

NGSS Lead States. (2013). *Next generation science standards: For states, by states*. Washington, DC: The National Academies Press.

O'Malley, P. J. (1982). Learn the truth about curriculum. *The Executive Educator, 4*(8), 14–26.

Ontario Principals' Council. (2008). *The principal as professional learning community leader*. Thousand Oaks, CA: Corwin.

Schmoker, M. (2011). *Focus: Elevating the essentials to radically improve student learning*. Alexandria, VA: ASCD.

Scott, B. E. (2012). *The effectiveness of differentiated instruction in the elementary mathematics classroom* (Doctoral dissertation). Retrieved from https://pdfs.semanticscholar.org/a19a/6695b43c4f5e415860121e1bf527b14ff861.pdf

Tomlinson, C. A. (1999). Mapping a route toward differentiated instruction. *Educational Leadership, 57*(1), 12–16.

Tomlinson, C. A. (2014). *The differentiated classroom: Responding to the needs of all learners*. Alexandria, VA: ASCD.

Tomlinson, C. A. (2017). *How to differentiate instruction in academically diverse classrooms* (3rd ed.). Alexandria, VA: ASCD.

Tomlinson, C. A., Moon, T., & Imbeau, M. B. (2015). *Assessment and student success in a differentiated* classroom [White paper]. Alexandria, VA: ASCD.

Treffinger, D. J., Hohn, R. L., & Feldhusen, J. F. (1979). *Reach each you teach: A handbook for teachers*. Buffalo, NY: D.O.K.

Webb, N. L. (1999). *Alignment of science and mathematics standards and assessments in four states*. Madison, WI: National Institute for Science Education.

Wiggins, G., & McTighe, J. (2005). *Understanding by design* (2nd. ed). Alexandria, VA: Association for Supervision and Curriculum Development.

Wolfe, P. (2001). *Brain matters: Translating research into classroom practice*. Alexandria, VA: Association for Supervision and Curriculum Development.

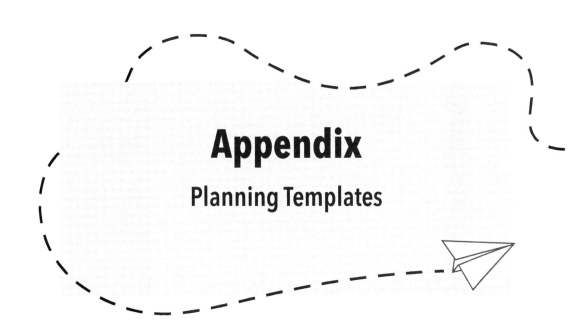

Appendix

Planning Templates

Concept-Based Instruction

Appendix 1
Full Unit Template

Continuous Literacy Skills Throughout the Year					
Literary Text Type					
Literature Standards					
Informational Text Standards					

Appendix 1, continued

Continuous Writing Skills Throughout the Year						
Literary Text Type						
Writing						
Speaking and Listening						

Concept-Based Instruction

Appendix 2
C3 Framework Template

This template may be used for repeated unit topics.

C3 Framework for Social Studies State Standards (Units reflect Dimension 2 and include a minimum of four areas.)	By the end of grade ____, individually and with others, students …			
	Civics *(Topic)*	**Economics**	**Geography**	**History** *(Topic)*
	Civic and Political Institutions	Economic Decision Making	Geographic Representations: Spatial Views of the World	Change, Continuity, and Context
	Participation and Deliberation: Applying Civic Virtues and Democratic Principles	Exchange and Markets	Human–Environment Interaction: Place, Regions, and Culture	Perspectives
		The National Economy		Historical Sources and Evidence
	Processes, Rules, and Laws	The Global Economy	Human Population: Spatial Patterns and Movements	Causation and Argumentation
			Global Interconnections: Changing Spatial Patterns	

Appendix 2, continued

Dimension (at least four with cross-connections as appropriate)	Civics	Economics	Geography	History
Culture				
Time, Continuity, and Change				
People, Places, and Environments				

Concept-Based Instruction

Dimension *(at least four with cross-connections as appropriate)*	Civics	Economics	Geography	History
Individual Development and Identity				
Individuals, Groups, and Institutions				
Power, Authority, and Governance				

Appendix 2, continued

Dimension (at least four with cross-connections as appropriate)	Civics	Economics	Geography	History
Production, Distribution, and Consumption				
Science, Technology, and Society				
Global Connections				
Civic Ideals and Practices				

Concept–Based Instruction © Taylor & Francis

Concept-Based Instruction

This template may be used for repeated unit topics.

Students who demonstrate understanding can:	By the end of grade ____, individually and with others, students . . .		
Dimension 1: Science and Engineering Practices • Asking questions (for science) and defining problems (for engineering) • Developing and using models • Planning and carrying out investigations • Analyzing and interpreting data • Using mathematics and computational thinking • Constructing explanations (for science) and designing solutions (for engineering) • Engaging in argument from evidence • Obtaining, evaluating, and communicating information			

Appendix 3, continued

Disciplinary Core Ideas • Physical Sciences • Life Sciences • Earth and Space Sciences • Engineering, Technology, and Application of Science			
Crosscutting Concepts • Patterns • Cause and effect • Scale, proportion, and quantity • Systems and system models • Energy and matter: Flows, cycles, and conservation • Structure and function • Stability and change			
Common Core State Standards Connections (ELA)			
Common Core State Standards Connections (Mathematics)			

131

Concept-Based Instruction

Topics	Concept-Based Themes	Core Ideas

Concept-Based Instruction © Taylor & Francis

Appendix 5
Thematic Brainstorming for Common Social Studies or Science Template

Science (across)	Social Studies (down)					

Appendix 6

Theme Brainstorming: Cross-Curricular Current Topics With Final Themes

Social Studies	Science	Language Arts
Theme:		
Theme:		
Theme:		

Concept-Based Instruction

	Social Studies	Science	Language Arts
Theme:			
Theme:			
Theme:			

Appendix 7

Topical Understandings, Standards, and Evidence of Learning Template

Topical Understandings	Common Core State Standards in English Language Arts	Evidence of Learning

Topical Understandings	C3 Framework for Social Studies State Standards	Evidence of Learning

Appendix 7, continued

Topical Understandings	Next Generation Science Standards	Evidence of Learning

Appendix 8
Single Theme Template

Theme	Social Studies	Science	Language Arts
	Know:	Know:	Know:
	Understand:	Understand:	Understand:
	Be able to do:	Be able to do:	Be able to do:

Concept-Based Instruction

Concept Theme:	Unit Name:		Dates:						
Essential Questions (3–5): 1. 2. 3. 4. 5.			Enduring Understandings: 1. 2. 3. 4. 5.						
Week of	Social Studies	Science	Literacy	Writing	Mathematics				

About the Author

Brian E. Scott, Ed.D., grew up in Warsaw, IN, and began his educational career in 1982 as a sixth-grade teacher in a small rural school. He has taught fourth, fifth, and sixth grades in a variety of configurations. He taught one year as a pull-out gifted and talented teacher and coached teachers to differentiate instruction for students in the general education classroom. He started his district's first multigrade, self-contained gifted and talented classroom before moving on to two different teaching assignments beginning in 1994, including a classroom of high-ability students clustered within the general education classroom.

In 2004 he was hired as an assistant principal and then as the principal in a suburban district just outside Indianapolis and served in that capacity before retiring from administration in 2016. He continued his studies and earned his Ed.D. from Ball State University in 2012. He came out of retirement and has served multiple educational roles as an adjunct professor, principal, and instructional coach.

Dr. Scott has been a presenter and consultant at the local, state, and national levels. He has created teacher workshops on active and engaging social studies, hands-on activities to enhance mathematics instruction, and high-yielding instructional strategies for creating a high-performing differentiated classroom.

For Product Safety Concerns and Information please contact our EU
representative GPSR@taylorandfrancis.com
Taylor & Francis Verlag GmbH, Kaufingerstraße 24, 80331 München, Germany

www.ingramcontent.com/pod-product-compliance
Ingram Content Group UK Ltd.
Pitfield, Milton Keynes, MK11 3LW, UK
UKHW031041080625
459435UK00013B/572